Be Inspired

I0502836

EYE TO EYE WITH THE TIGER

A REALISTIC ADULT COLOURING BOOK
THAT SHARES SOME AMAZING FACTS

*Thank You For Purchasing this Book, and We Hope
You Enjoy the Adventure of Stunning Grayscale
and B&W Colouring Pages of These Magnificent
Creatures to Bring into Full Life.
Created Especially For the Brave Hearted
And Compassionate Who Appreciate
The Powerful Beauty of the Tiger*

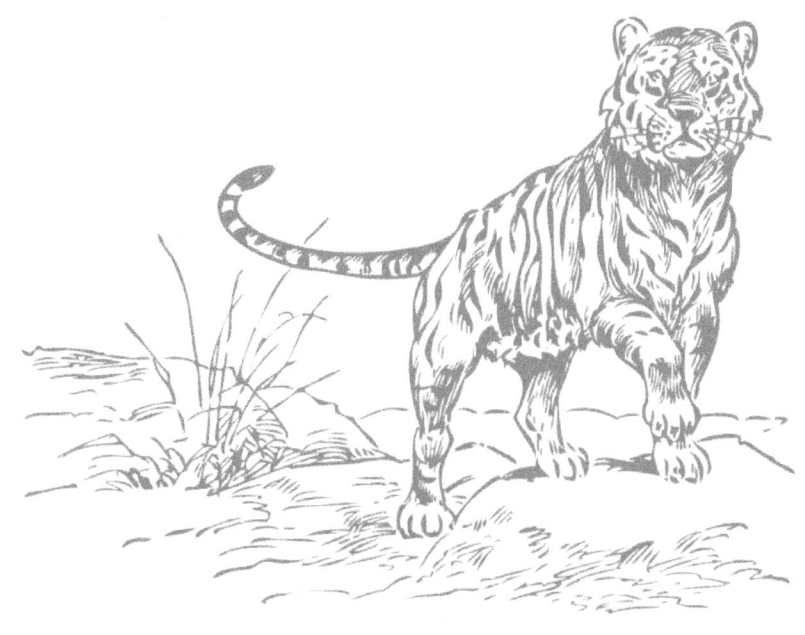

Copyright 2023 VOW-Voice of Wisdom ©

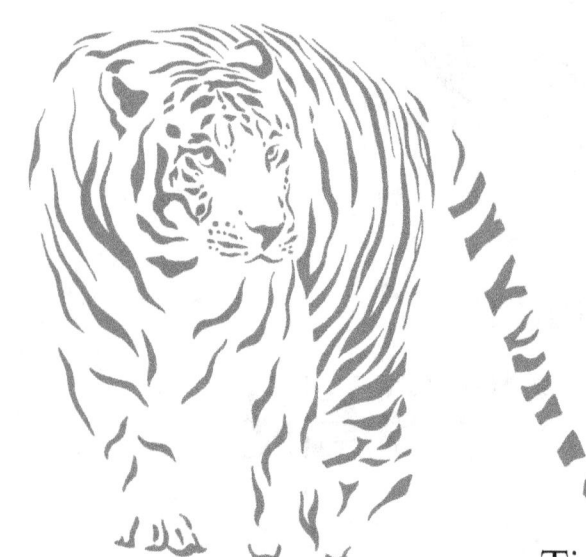

"The most magnificent creature in the entire world, the tiger is."
— Jack Hanna

Tigers are majestic creatures, with their striking stripes and powerful presence.

These big cats are a symbol of strength, beauty, and grace, and have captured our imaginations for centuries.

But tigers are more than just symbols. They are important to the ecosystems they inhabit, playing a crucial role in maintaining the balance of their habitats. As apex predators, they keep prey populations in check and help to prevent overgrazing and other environmental problems.

Despite their importance, tigers are endangered. Their populations have declined dramatically in recent years due to habitat loss, poaching, and other human activities and with only approximately 3,900 Tigers left in the wild globally.

It's up to us to be aware and protect these magnificent animals and ensure that they continue to thrive in the wild.

One way to celebrate the beauty and majesty of tigers is through art.

Adult coloring books provide a perfect opportunity to appreciate the intricate details of these big cats and bring them to life with color.

As you color in these hyper-realistic images of tigers, take a moment to appreciate their unique beauty and the important role they play in our world. Let the intricate patterns of their fur and the intensity of their gaze inspire you to create a work of art that captures the essence of these amazing creatures.

Through your art, you can help to raise awareness about the importance of protecting tigers and their habitats. So grab your colored pencils or markers and start creating a masterpiece that celebrates the majesty and beauty of these magnificent animals.

Copyright 2023 VOW-Voice of Wisdom ©

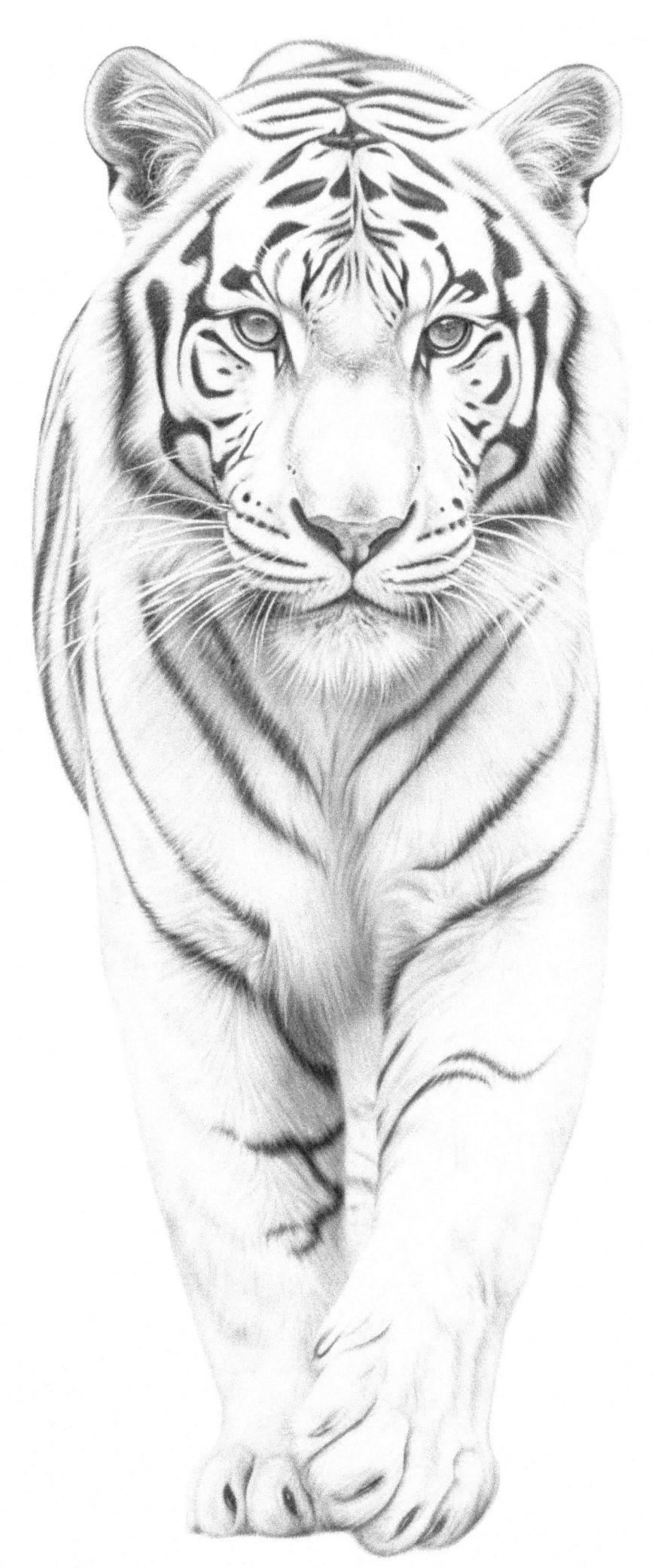

"
Tigers are the largest cats in the world. They can weigh up to 600 pounds and grow up to 10 feet long, including their tail

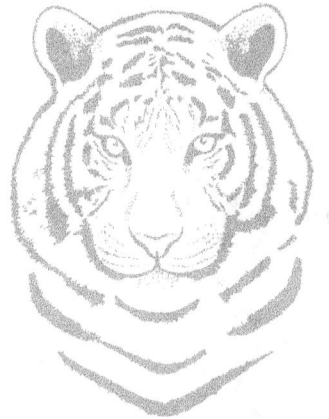

"

Have a fearless heart like a Tiger

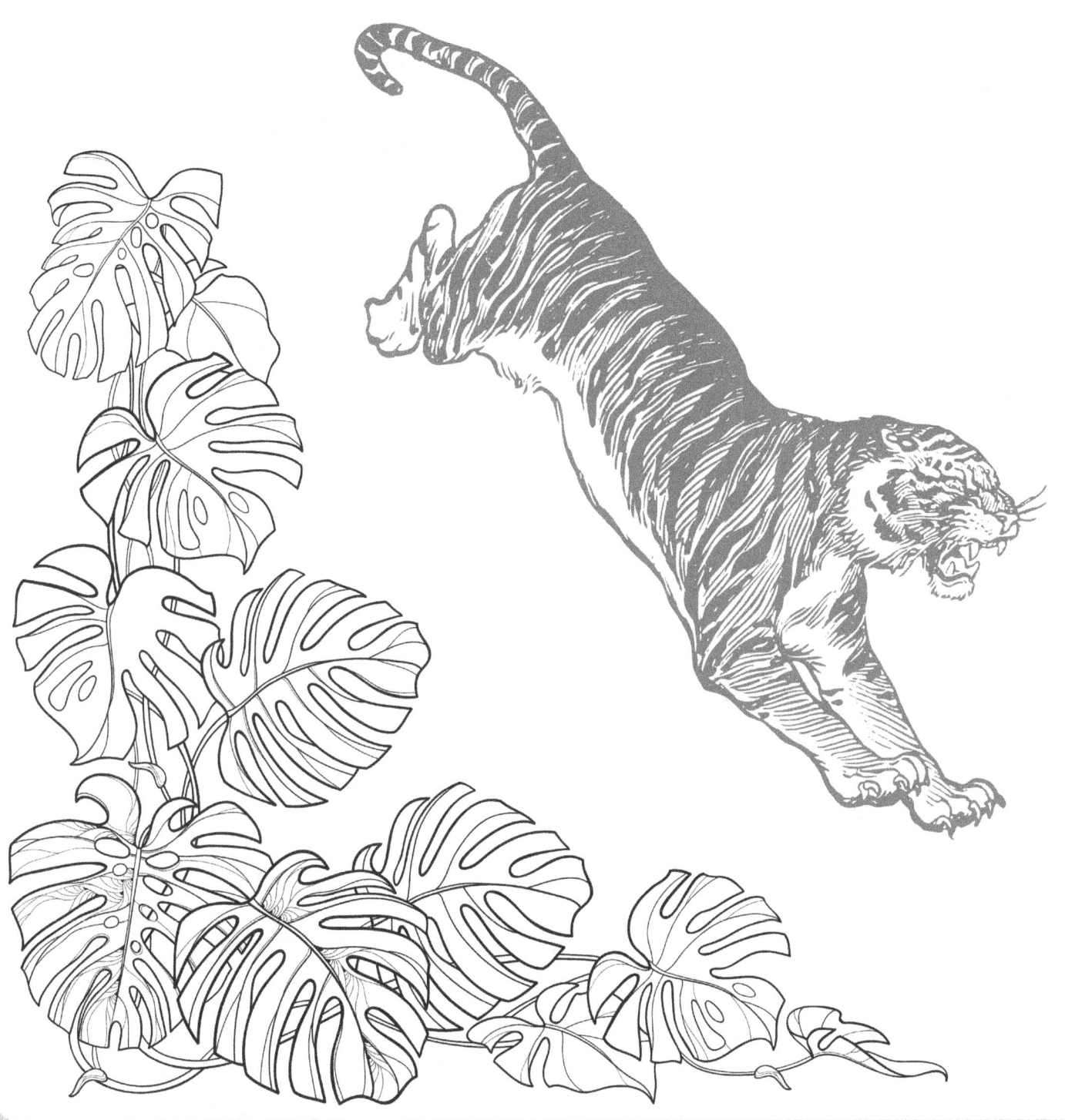

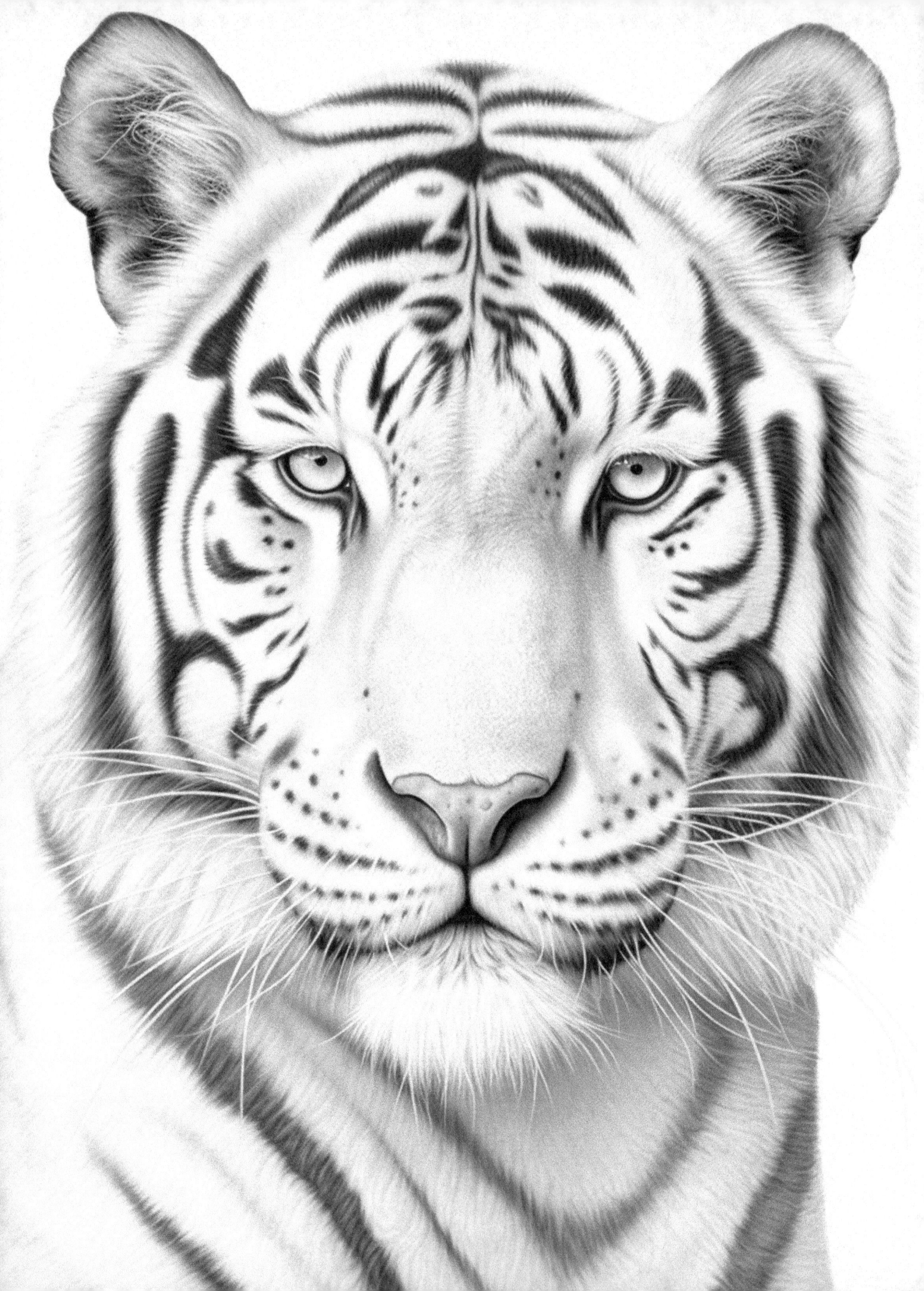

"

There are only
around 3,900 wild
tigers left in the
world.

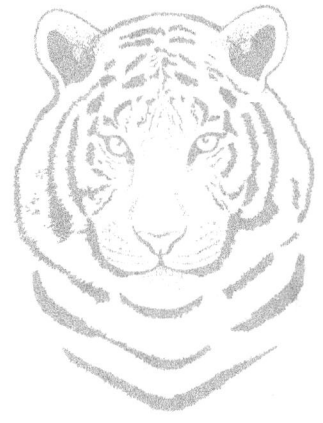

"

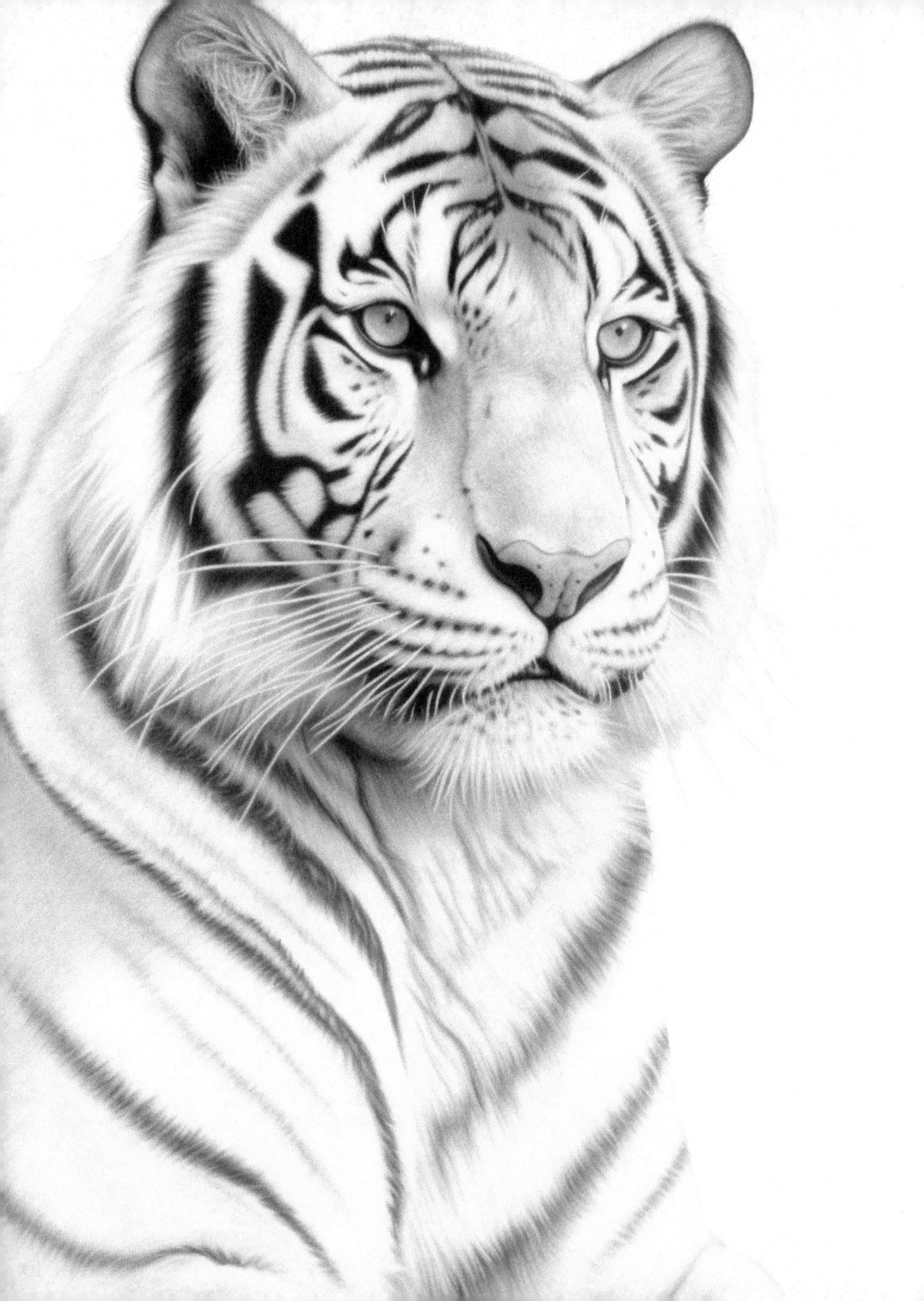

> "Tiger stripes are unique to each individual and help them camouflage in their environment."

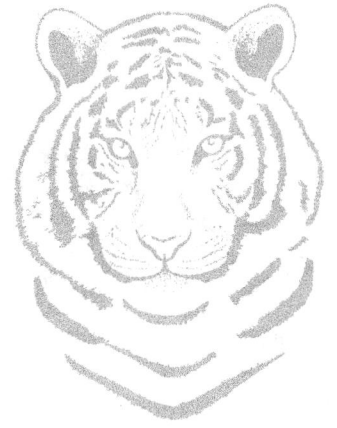

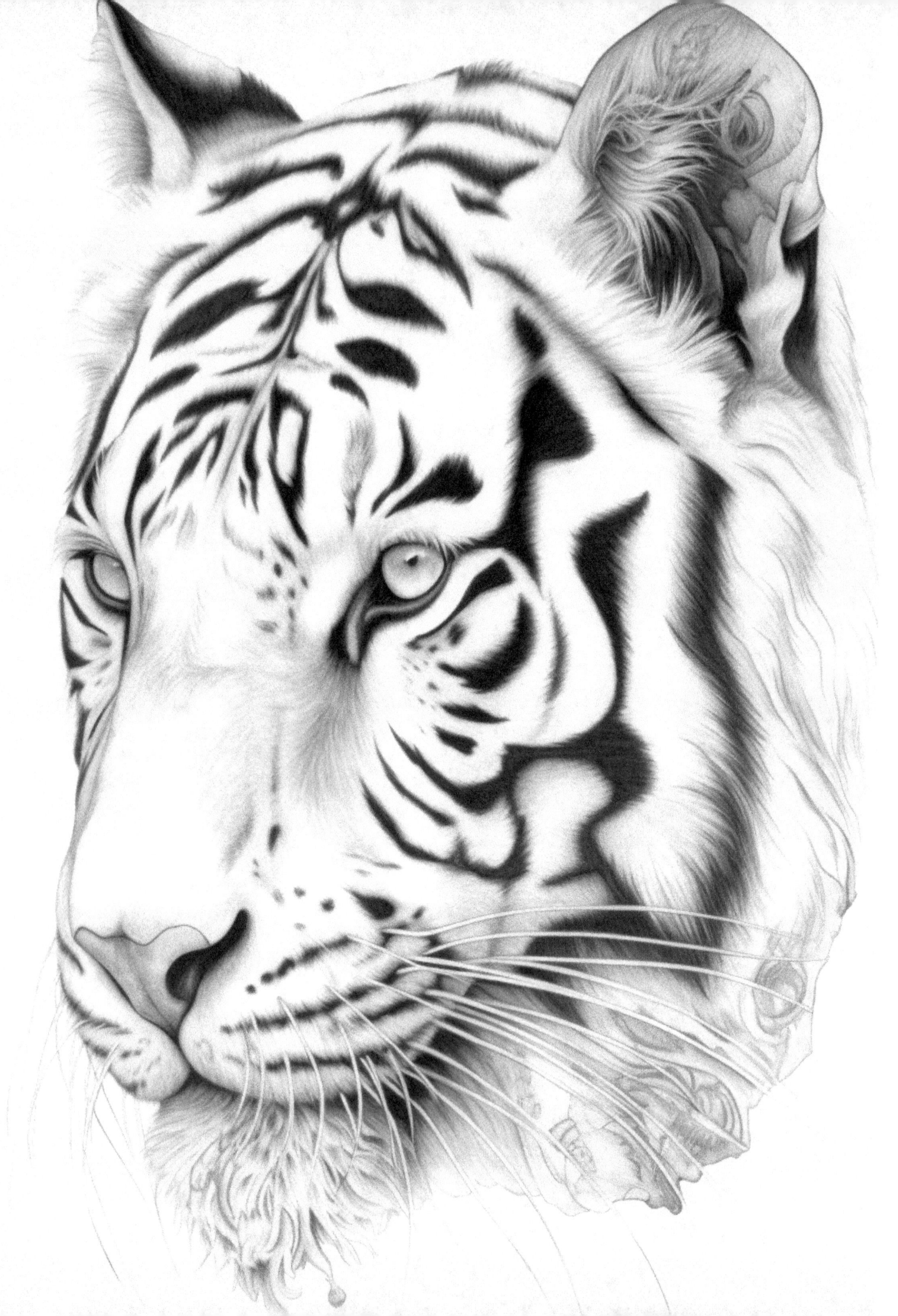

"

Tigers are excellent
swimmers and can
swim up to 3 miles
without stopping.

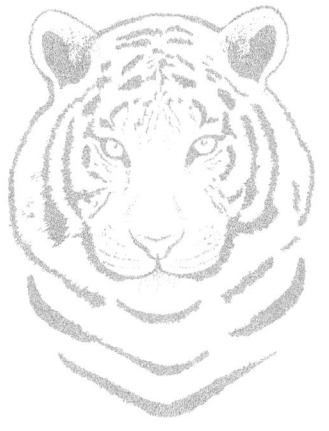

"

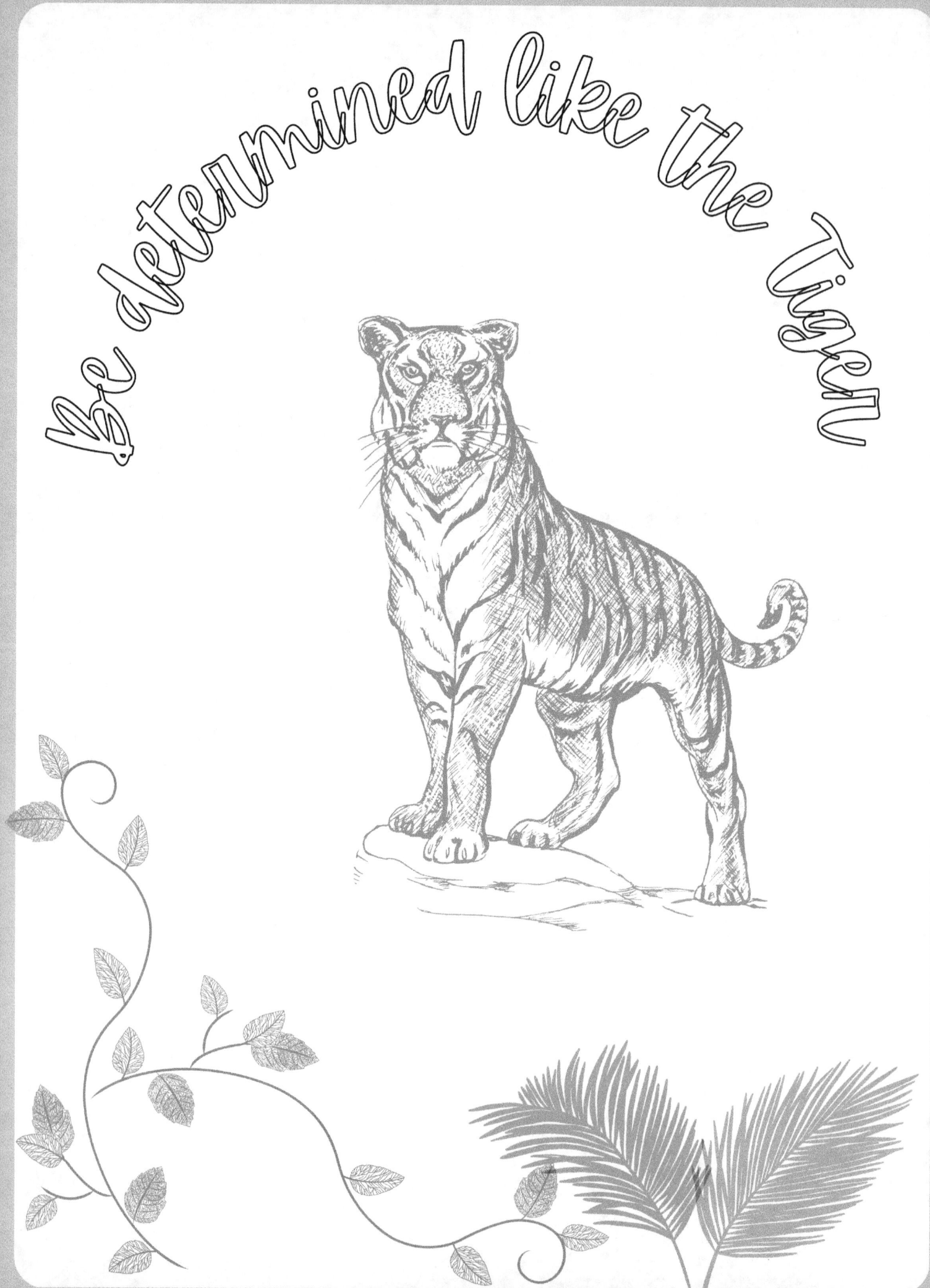

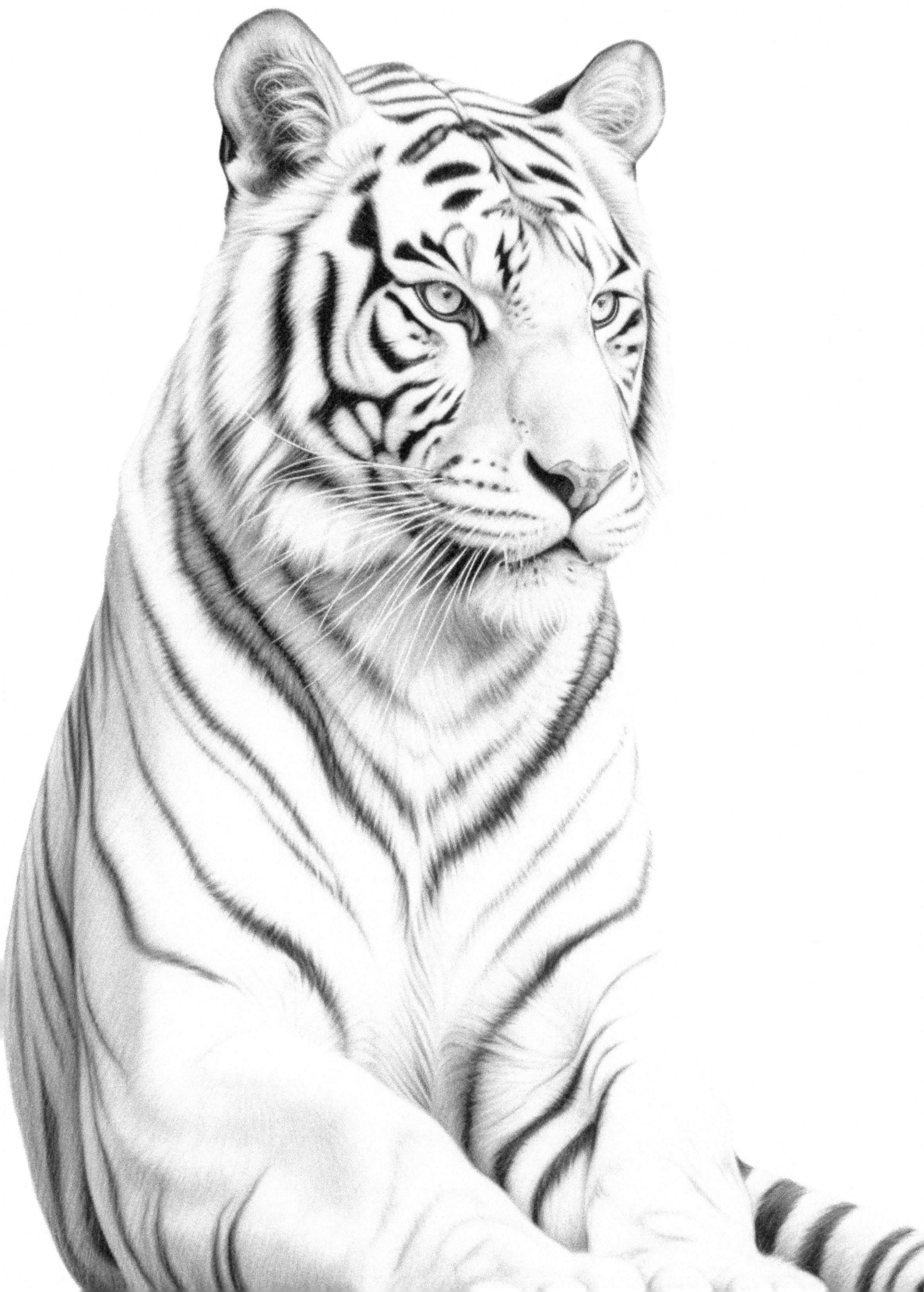

> The roar of a tiger can be heard up to 2 miles away.

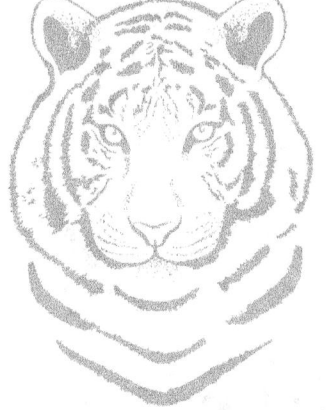

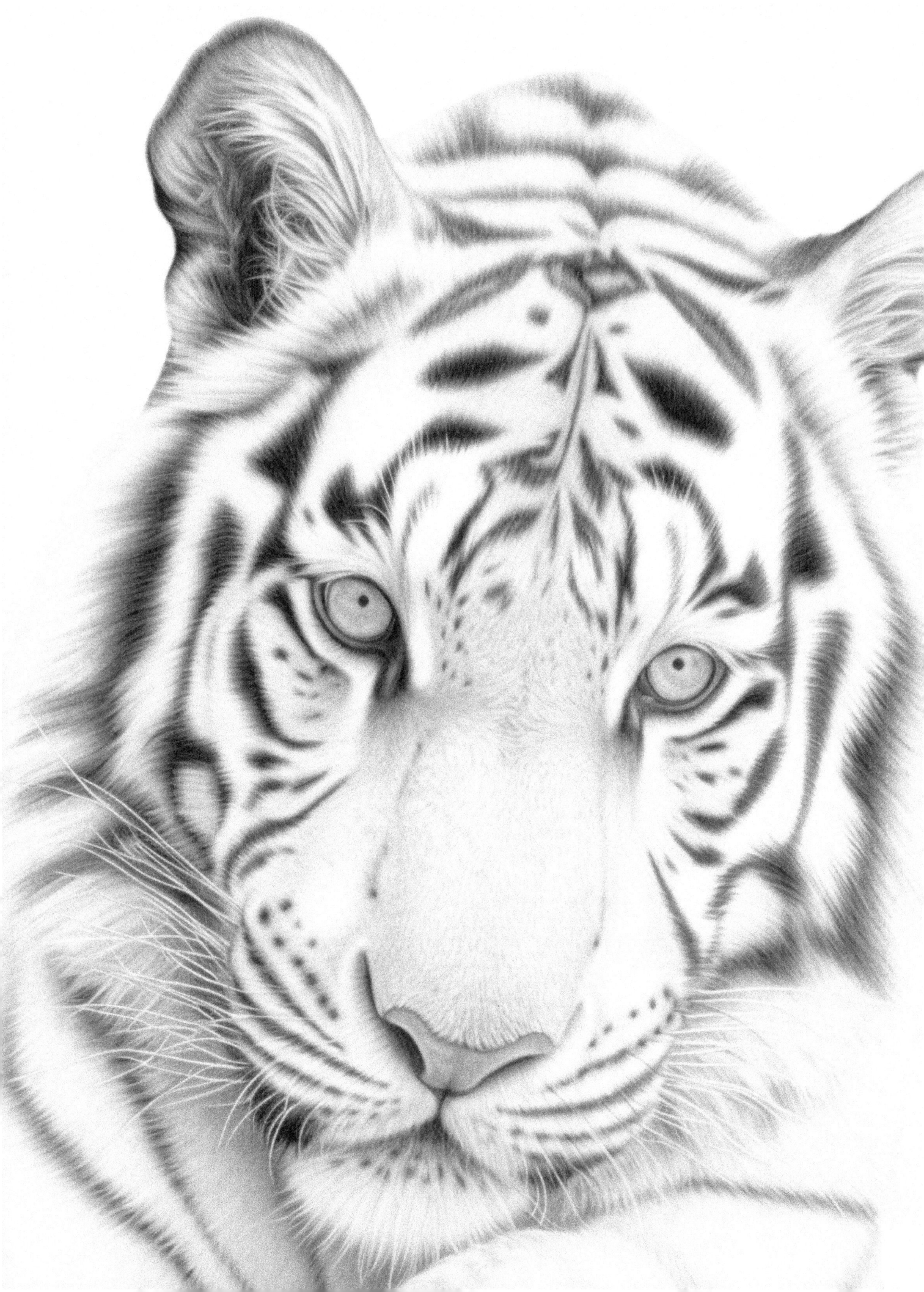

> Sadly Tigers have been hunted for their fur and body parts, which are used in traditional Eastern medicine.

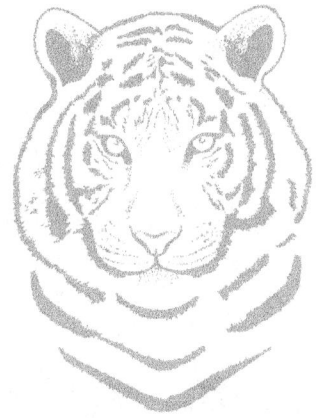

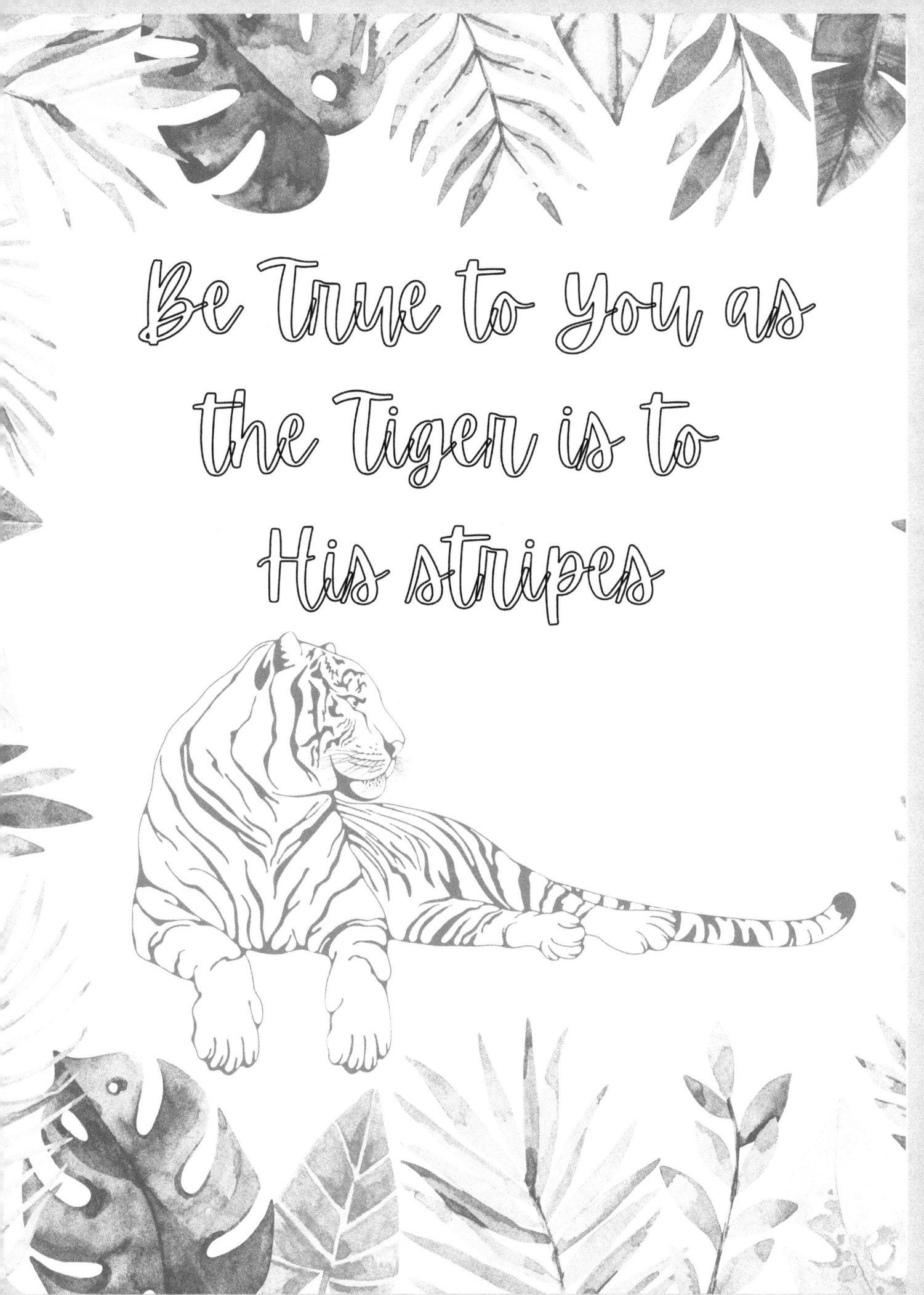

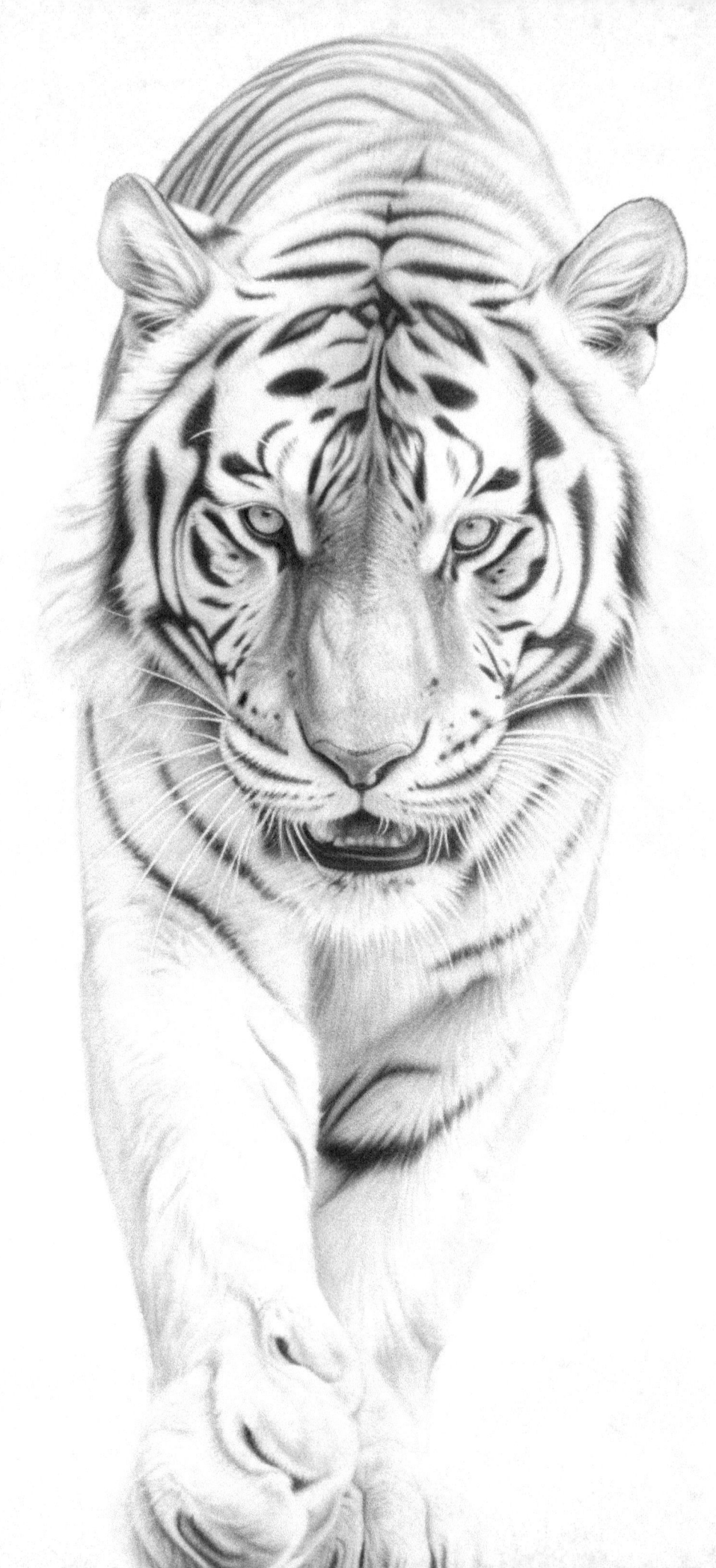

66

Tigers have a flexible
spine that allows them to
twist and turn in mid-air
when leaping.

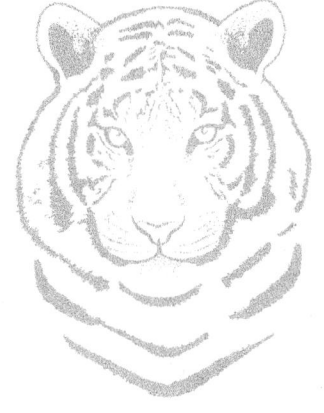

99

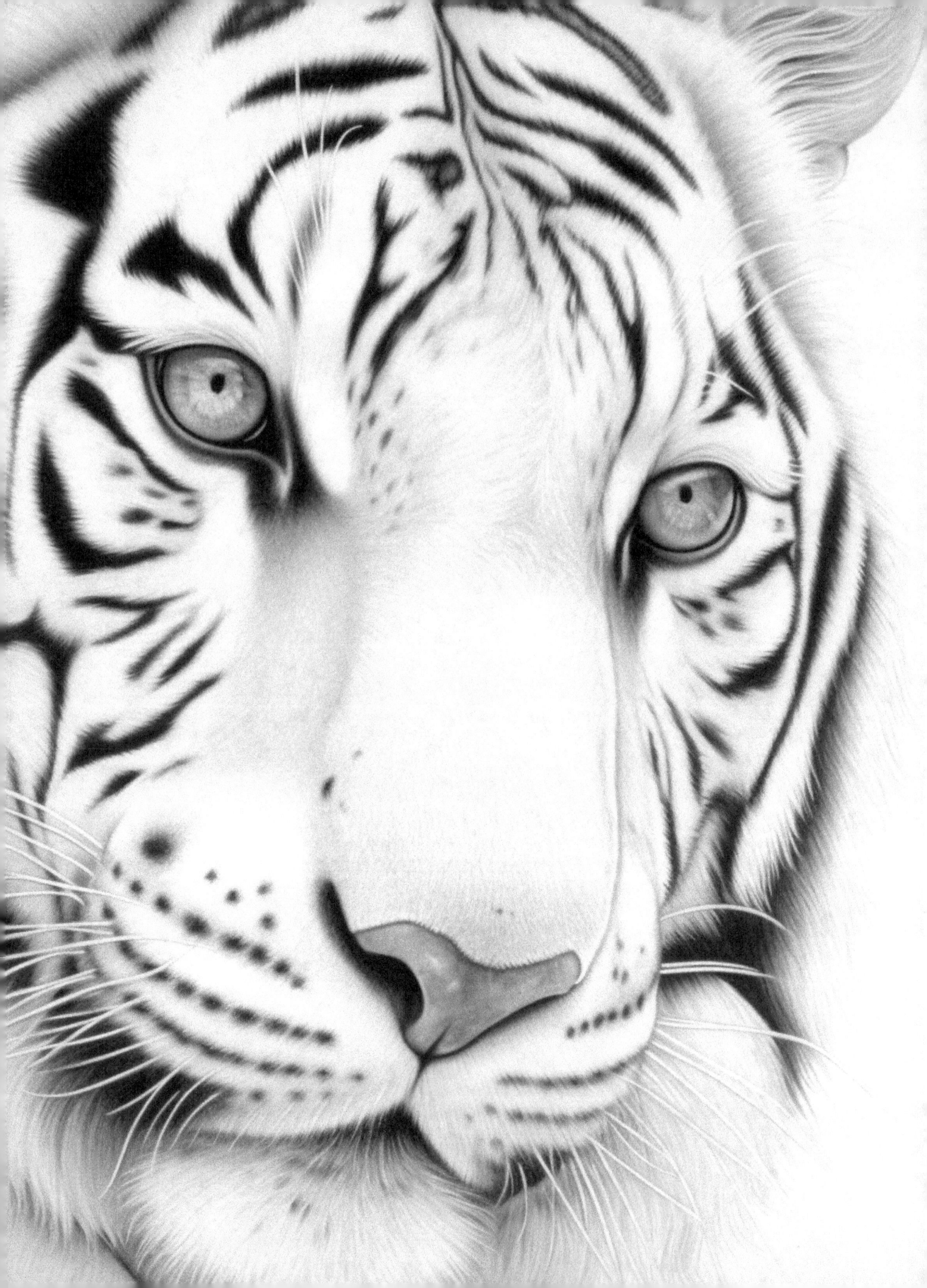

"

Tigers can run up to 35 miles per hour and they have retractable claws, which help them climb trees and catch prey.

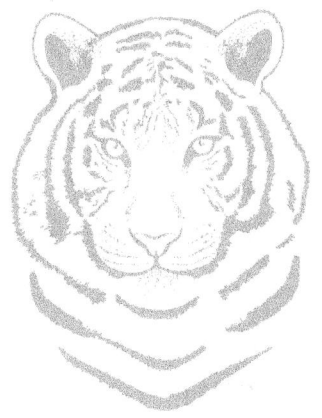

"

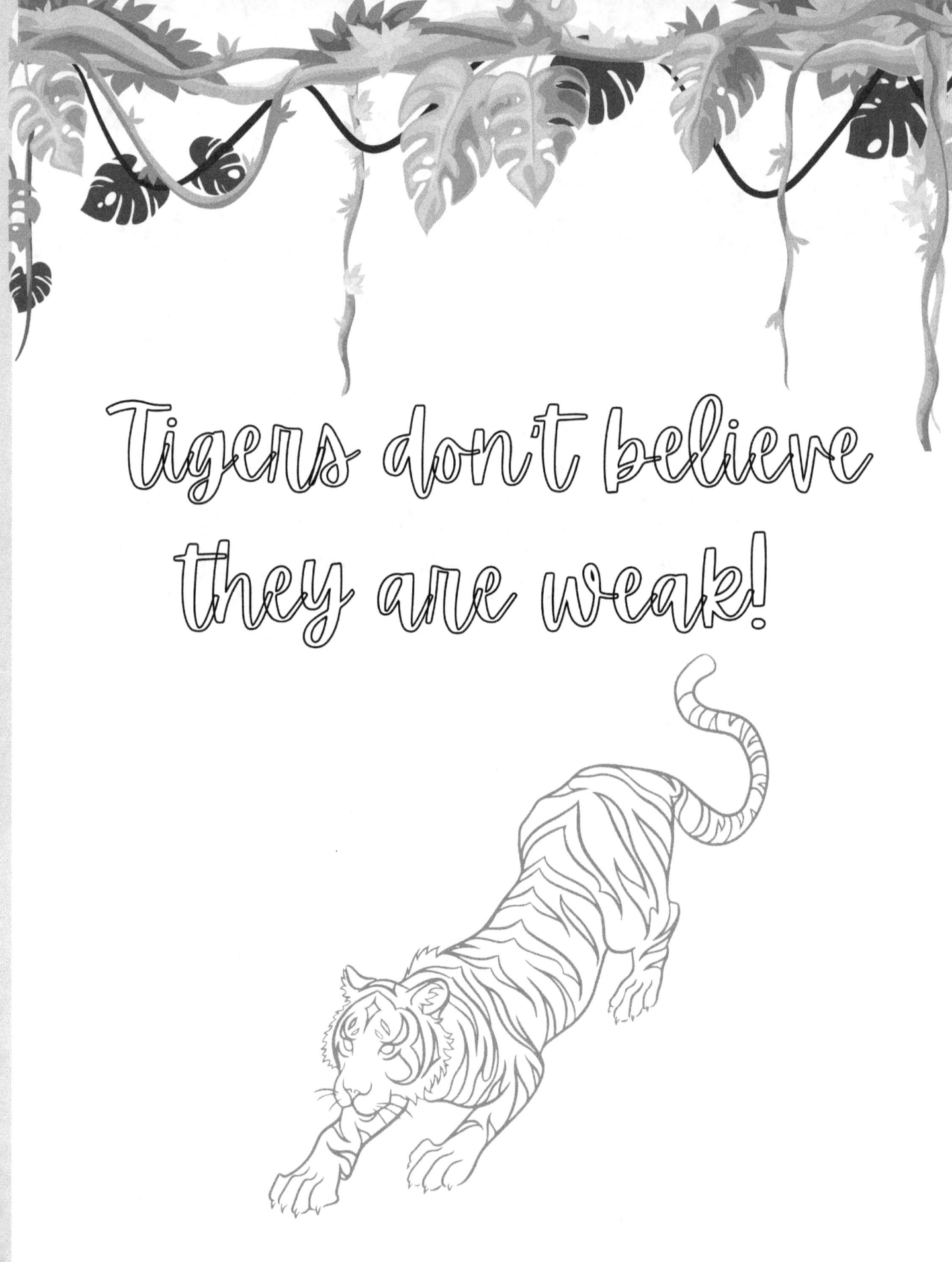

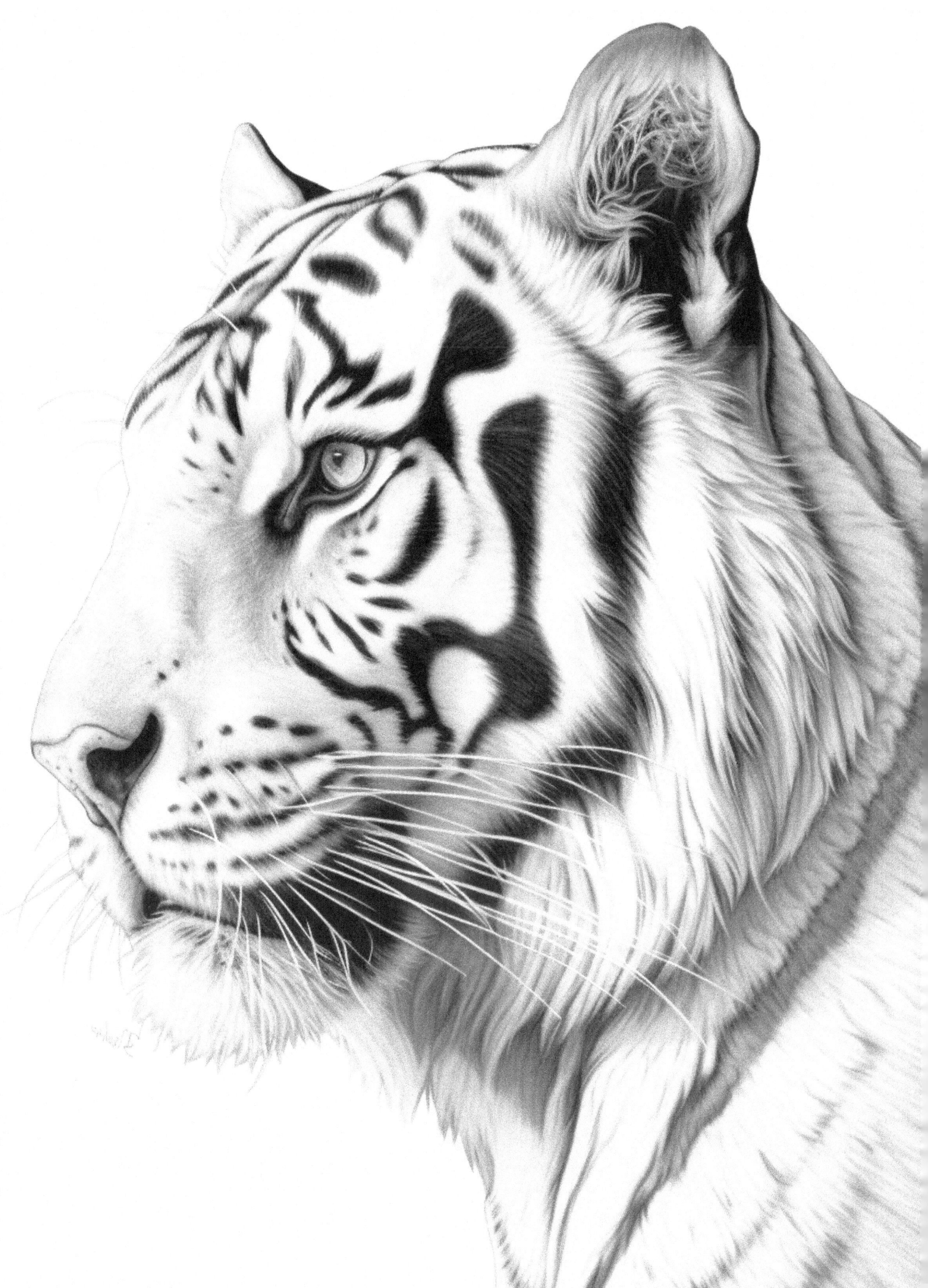

> The stripes on a tiger's
> fur are not only on their
> fur but also on
> their skin.

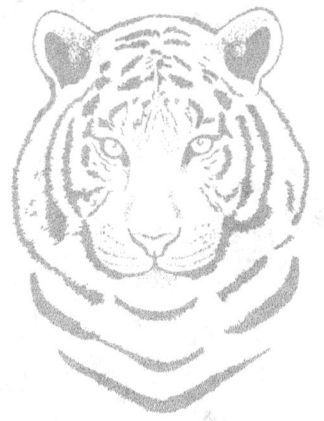

Pay attention. Winning opportunites are all around if hunt like a tiger!

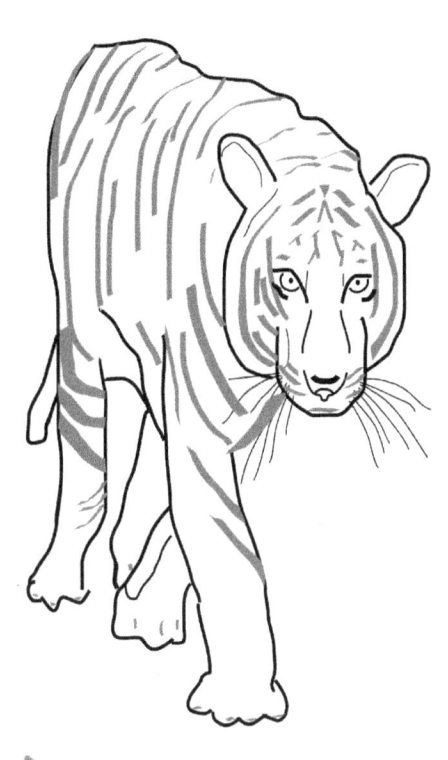

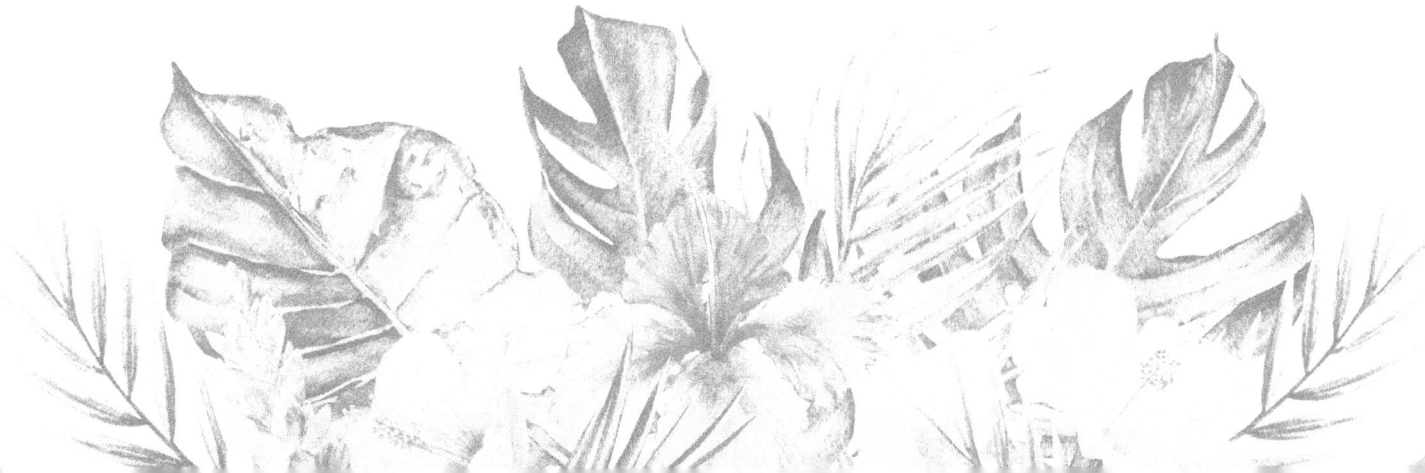

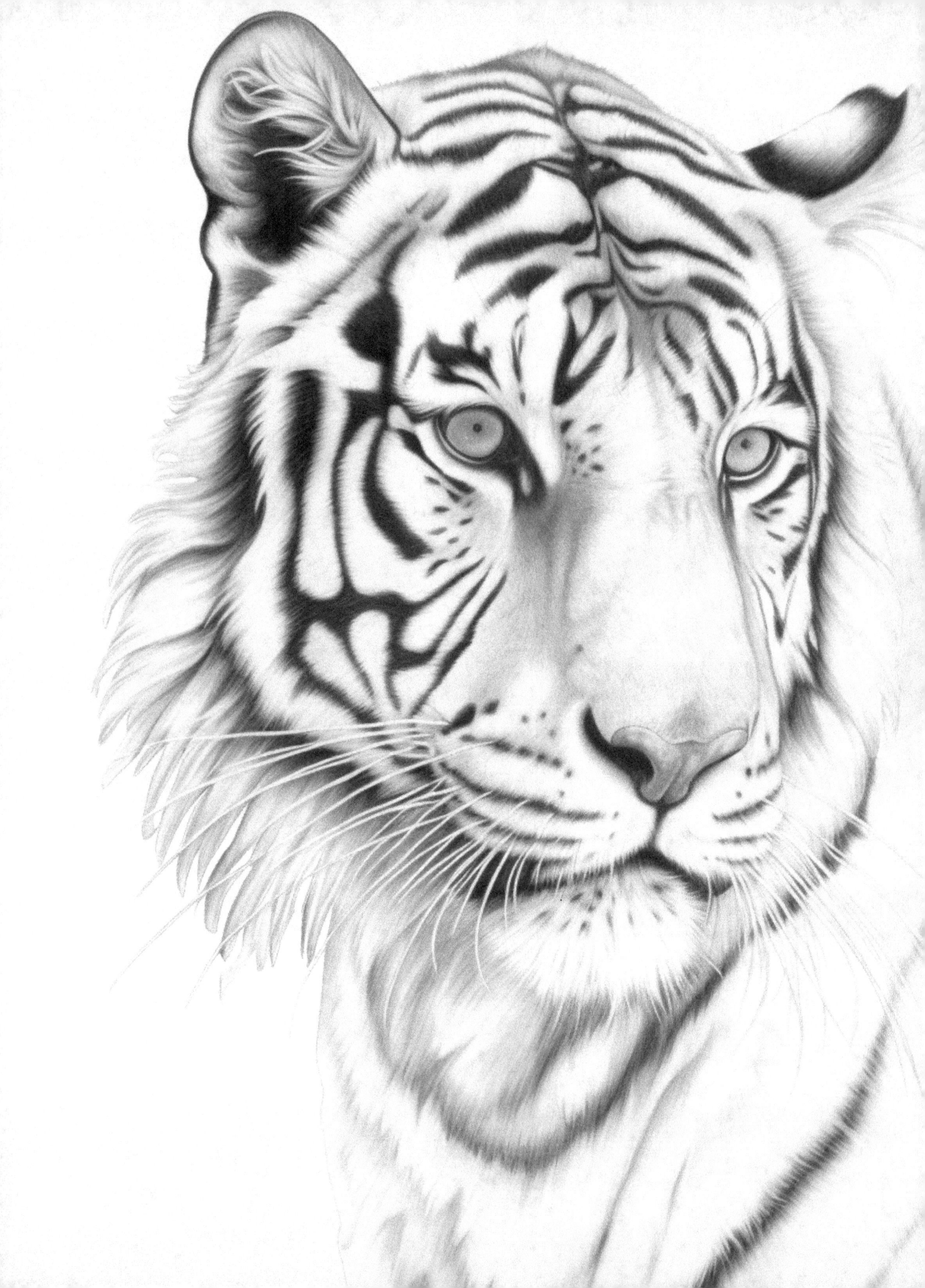

> Tigers have excellent hearing and can detect the sound of prey up to a mile away.

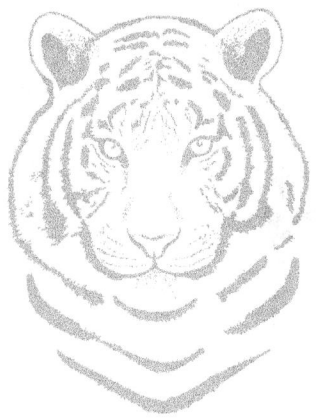

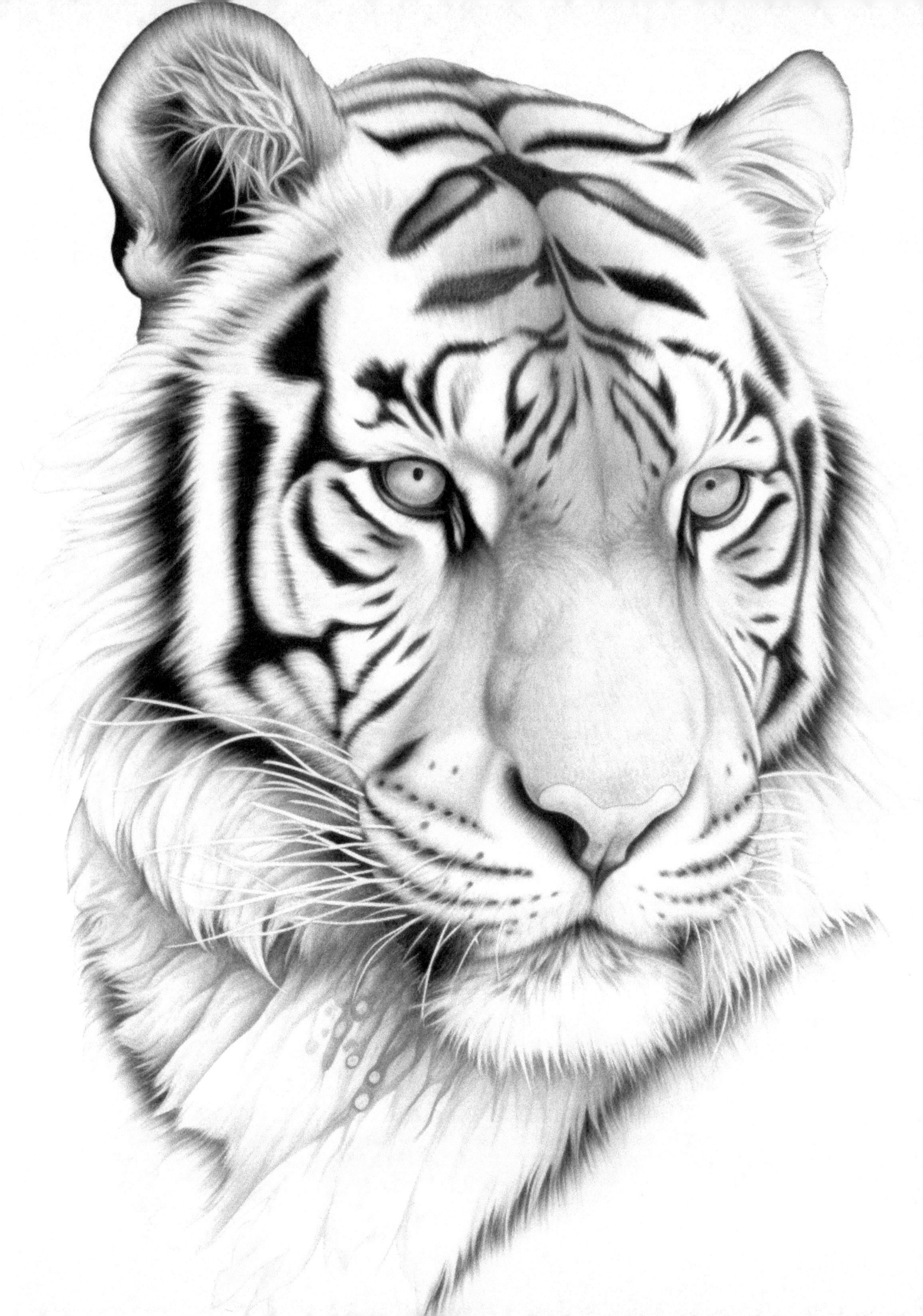

" Tigers have a lifespan of around 10-15 years in the wild and up to 20 years in captivity.

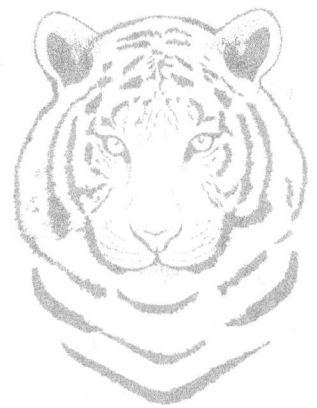

"

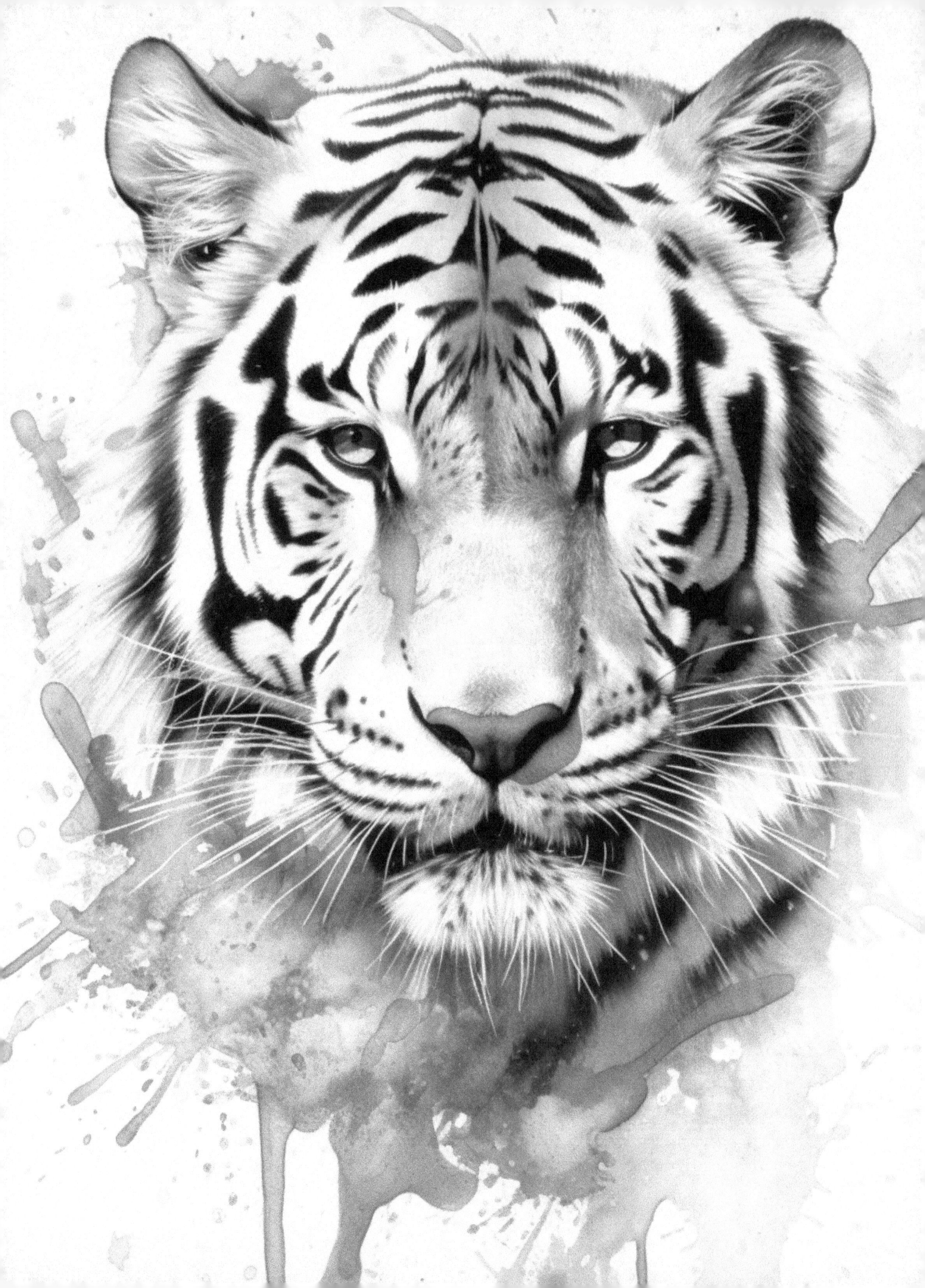

" The white tiger is a rare
genetic mutation of the
Bengal tiger and is not a
separate subspecies. "

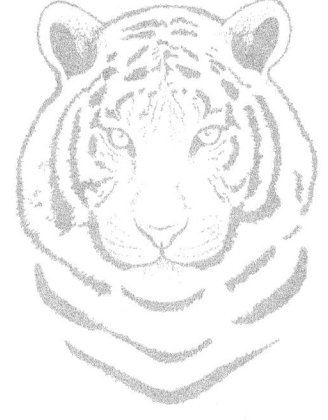

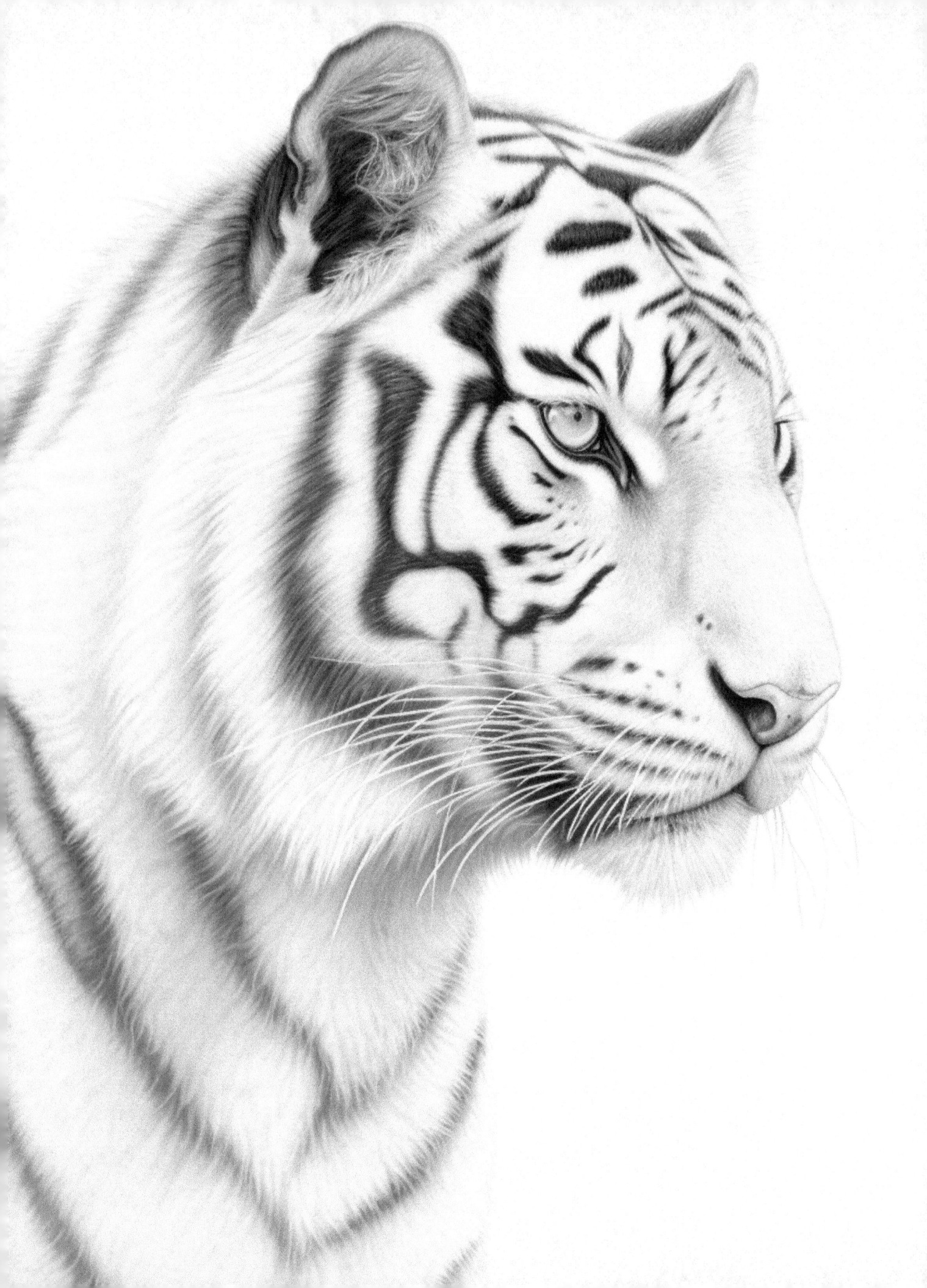

> "Like a human fingerprint, no two tigers have the same pattern of stripes on their coats. Scientists can use these distinctions to identify tigers in the wild."

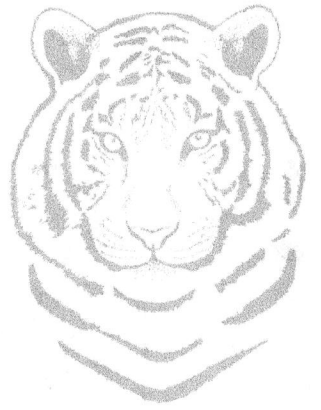

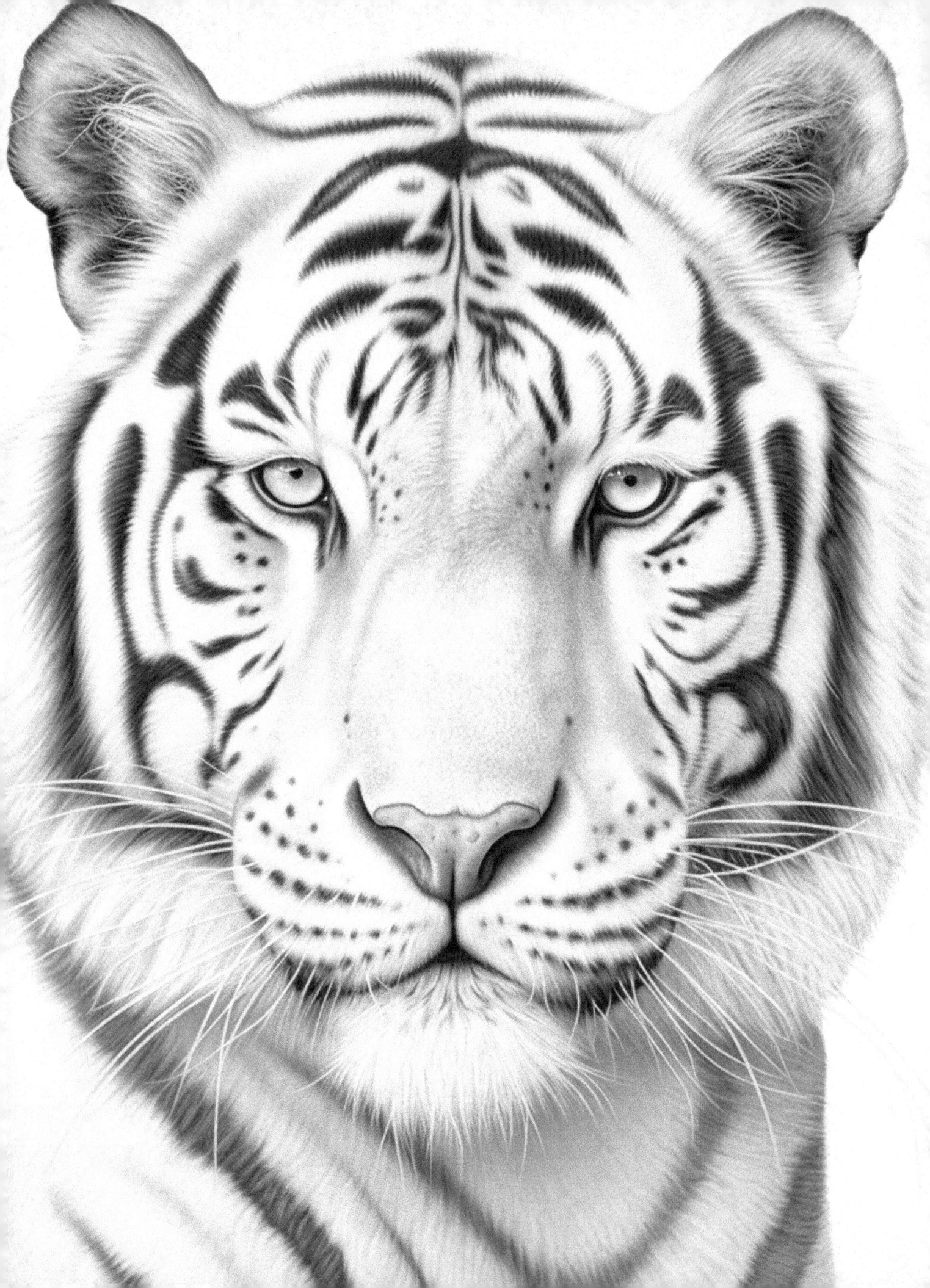

"

Tiger populations have
declined by around 95%
over the past century
due to human activity.

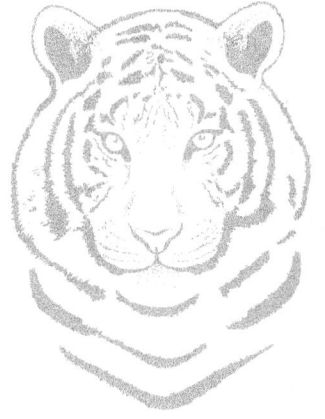

"

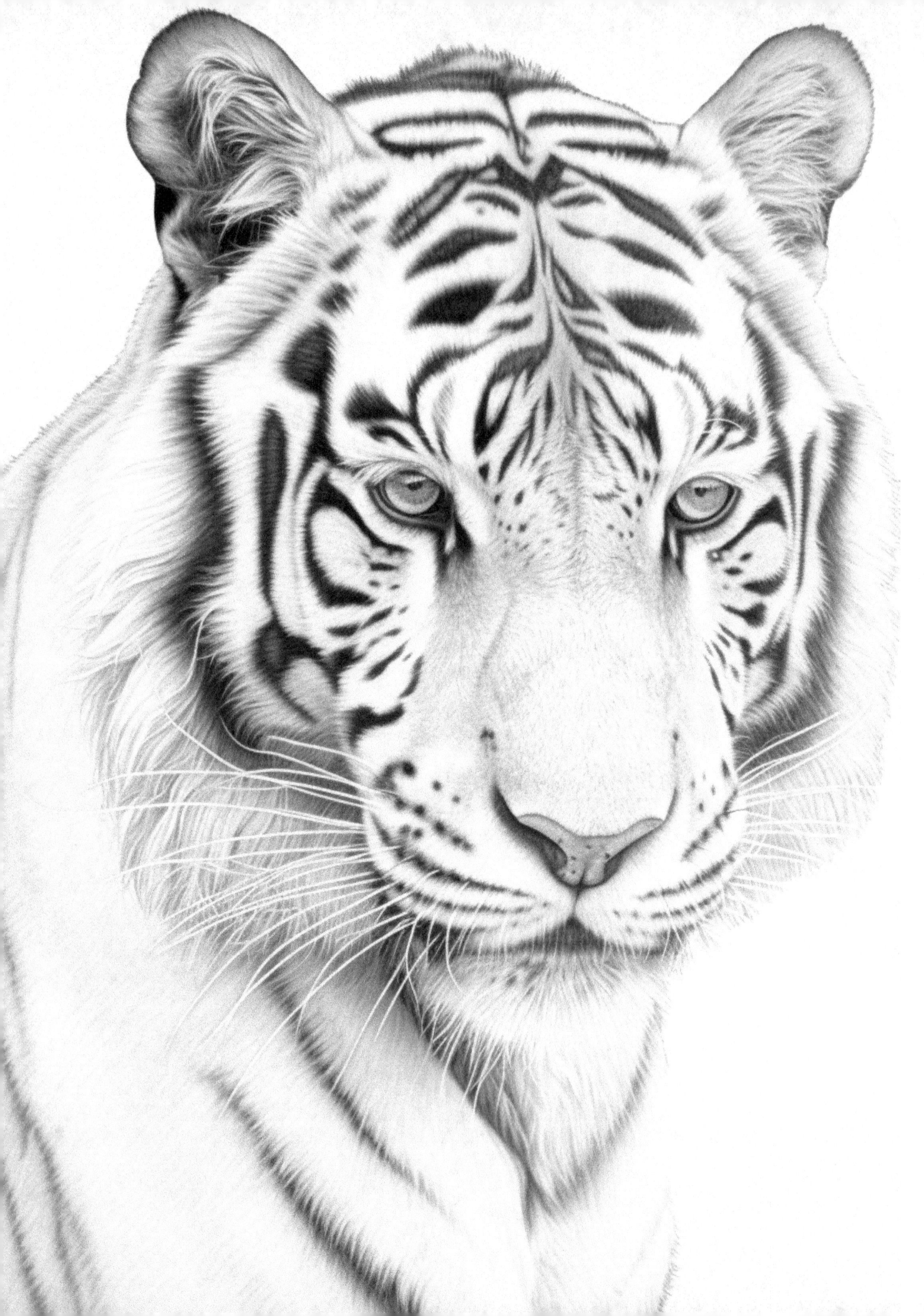

" "

Tigers have a special
adaptation in their
throats called a laryngeal
pad, which allows them
to make their distinctive
growling sound.

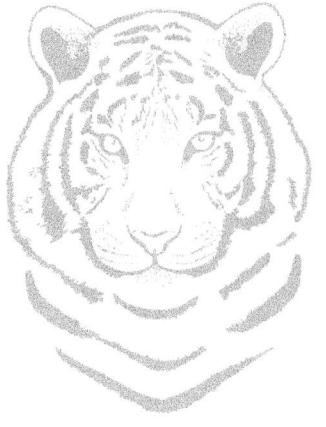

" "

Find your inner tiger to succeed!

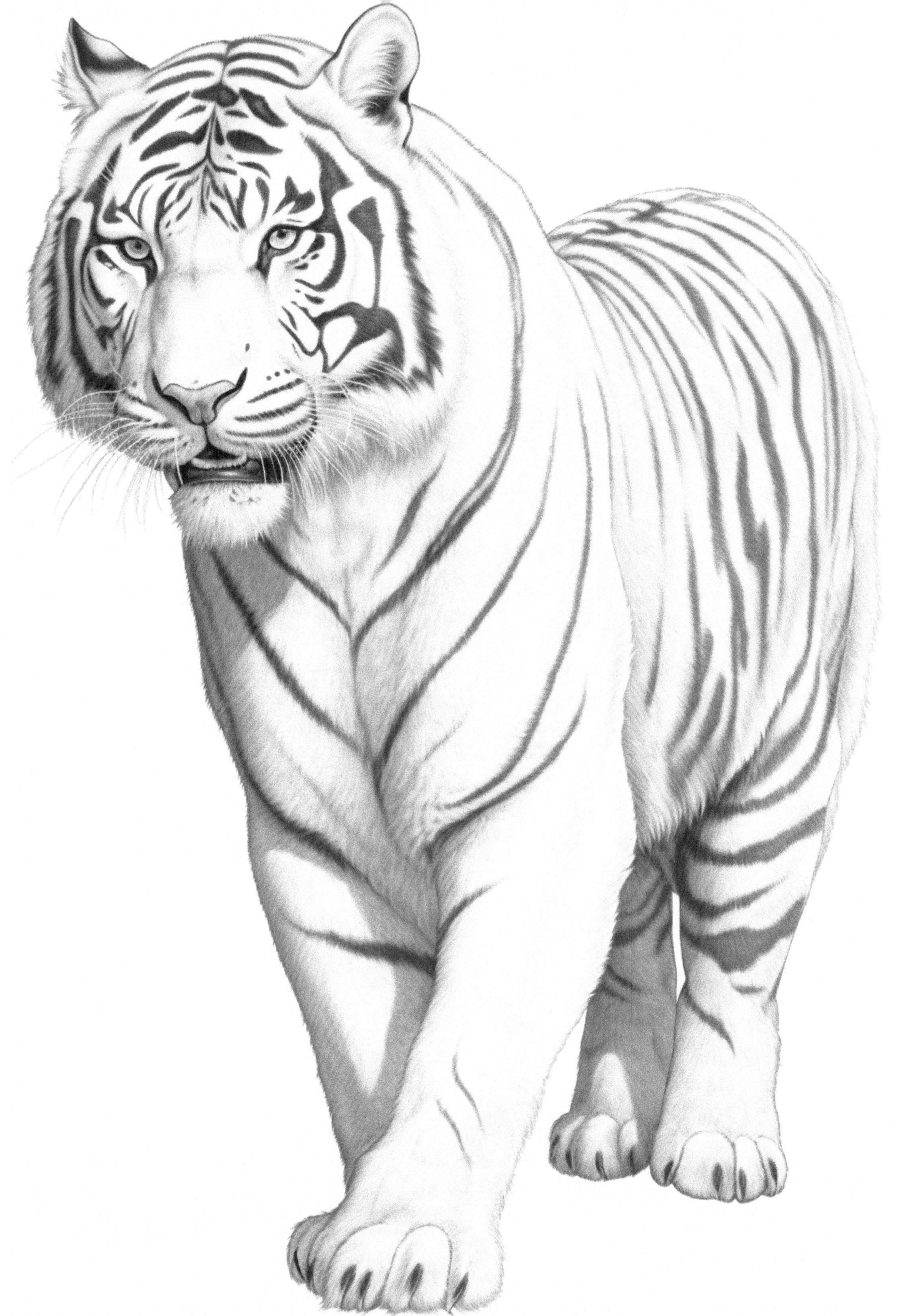

> Tigers can use their ears to communicate. A tigress uses the white spots on the back of her ears to communicate with her cubs.

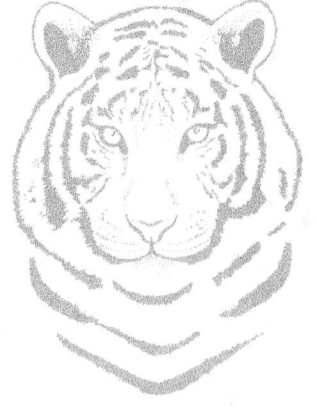

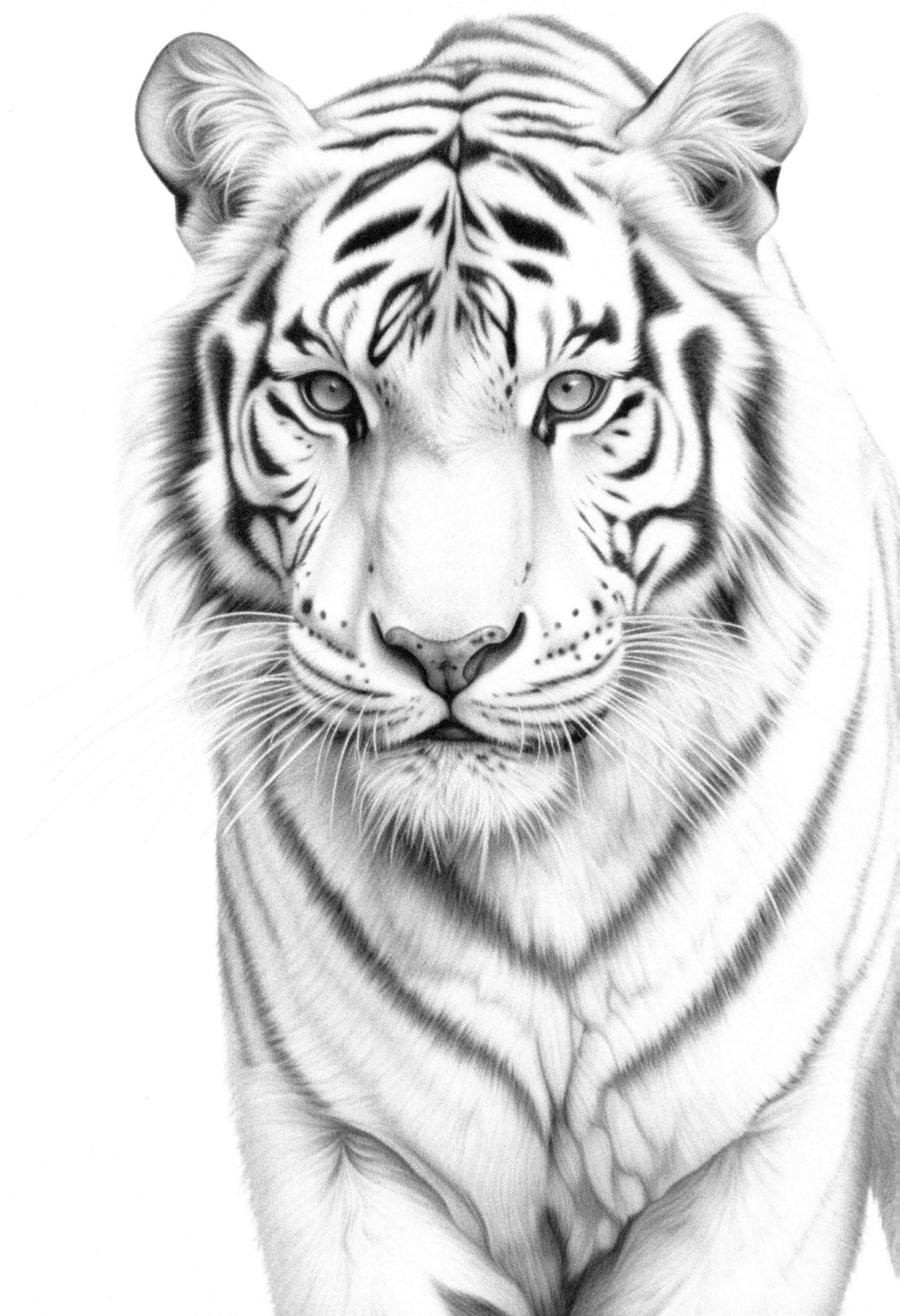

> Tigers can use their ears to communicate. A tigress uses the white spots on the back of her ears to communicate with her cubs.

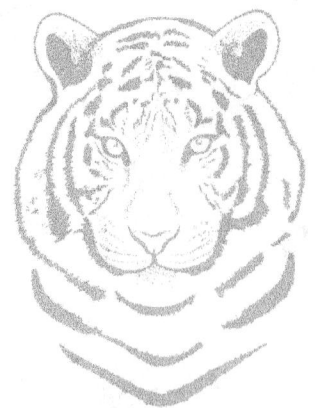

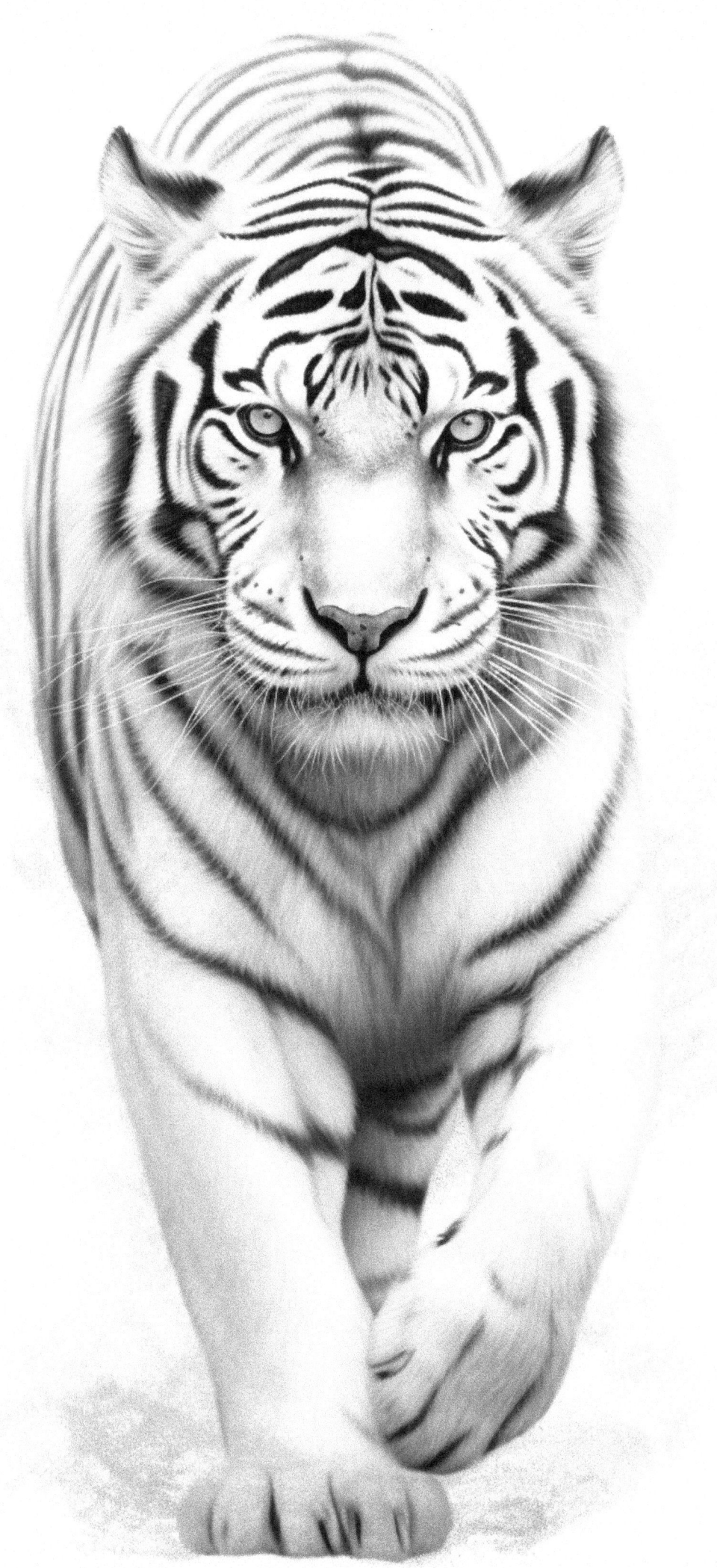

> Tigers are apex predators and are at the top of the food chain in their ecosystem.

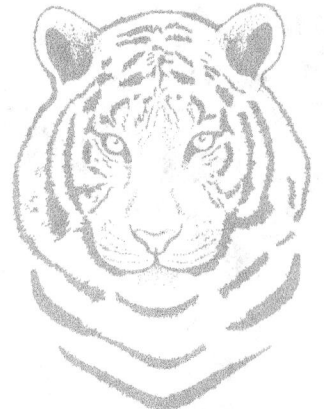

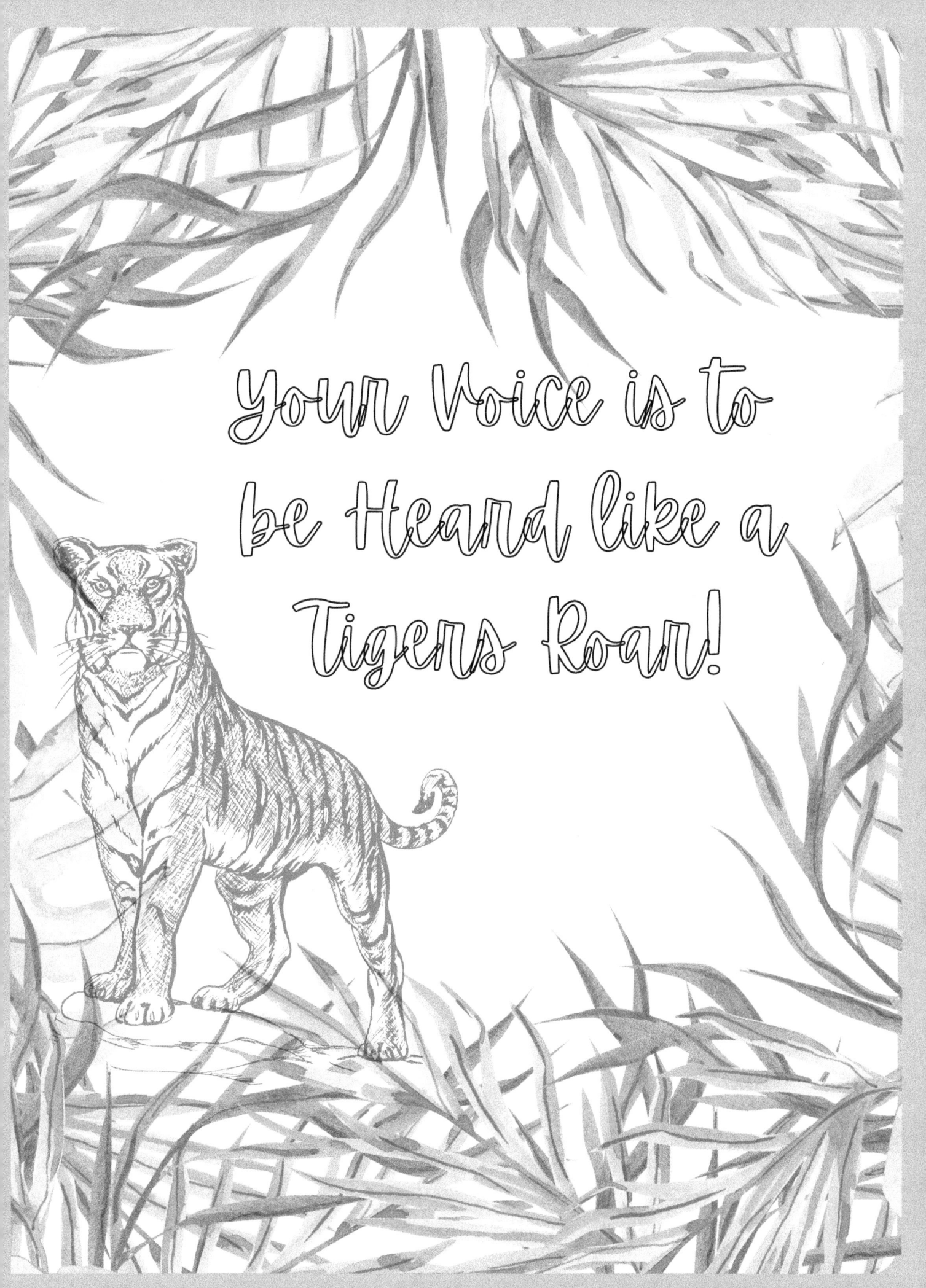

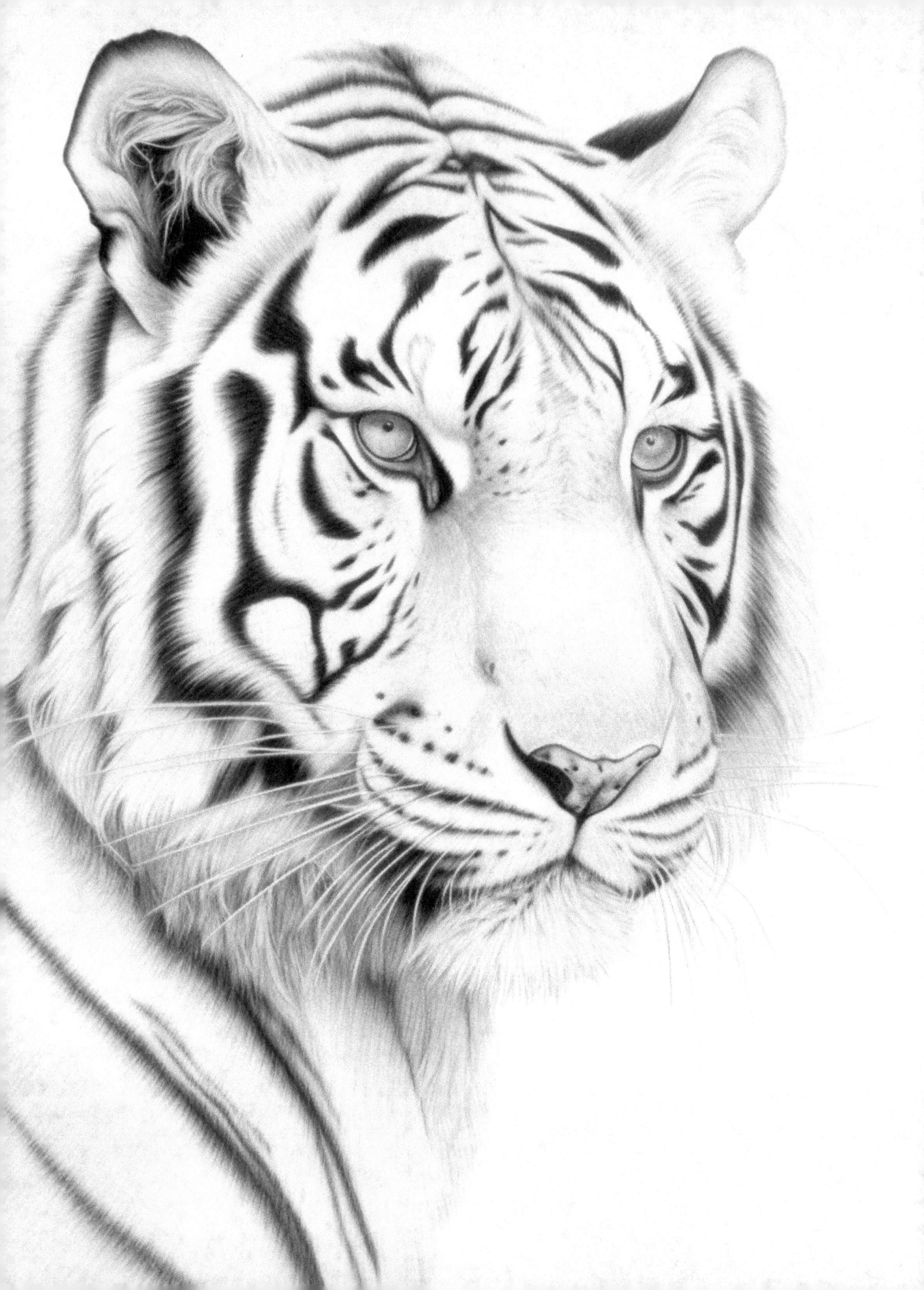

" Tigers are the largest cats in the world. They are carnivores and primarily eat large prey like deer, wild boar, and buffalo. "

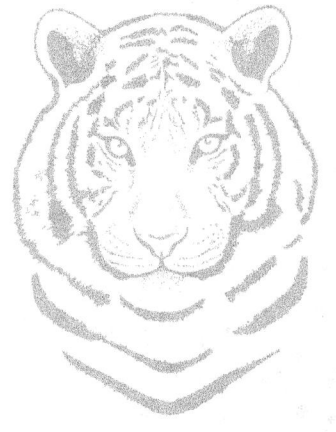

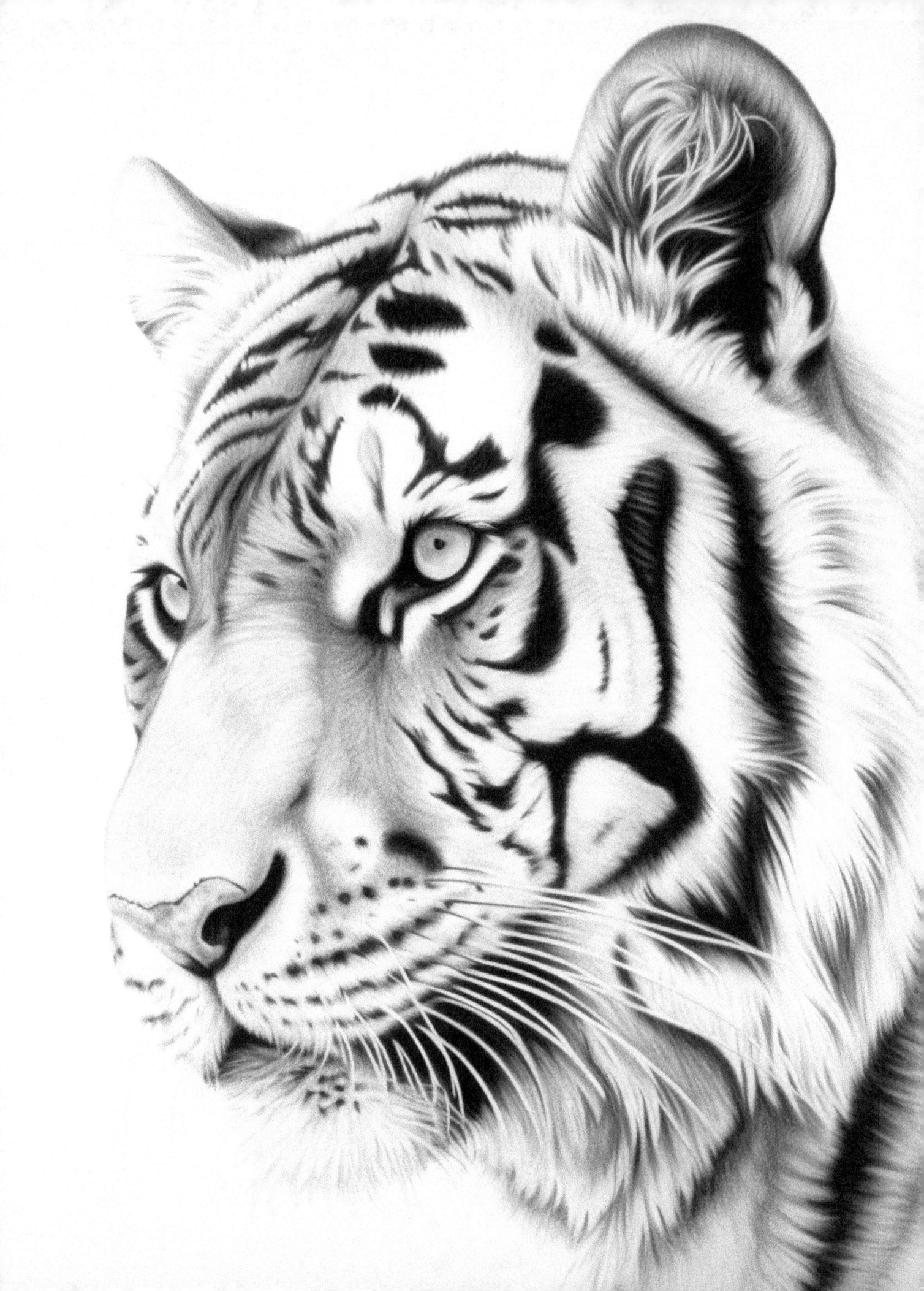

> Tigers have a lifespan of around 10–15 years in the wild and up to 20 years in captivity.

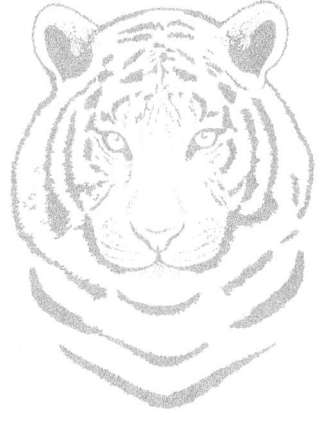

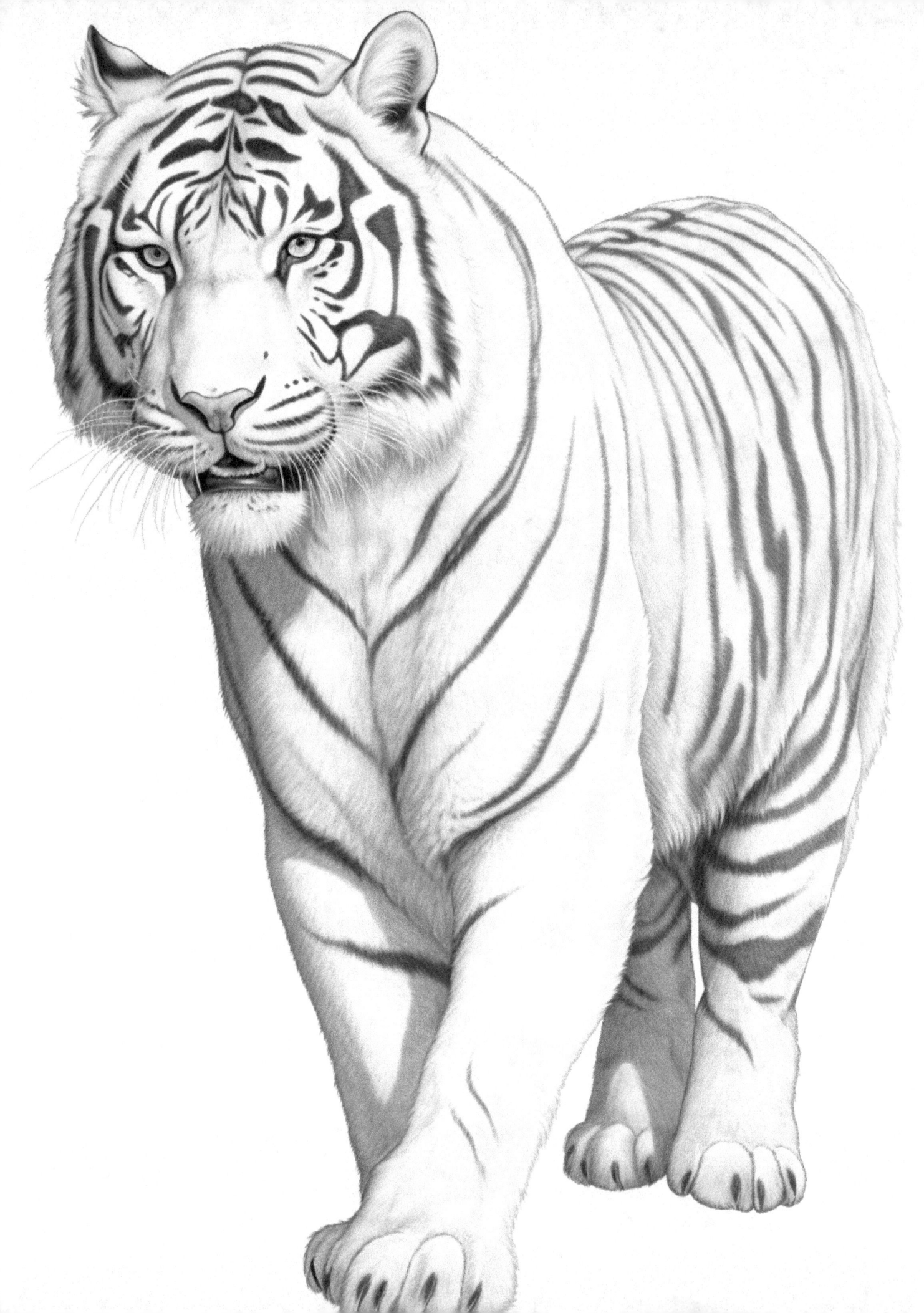

> Tigers are the largest cats in the world. They are carnivores and primarily eat large prey like deer, wild boar, and buffalo.

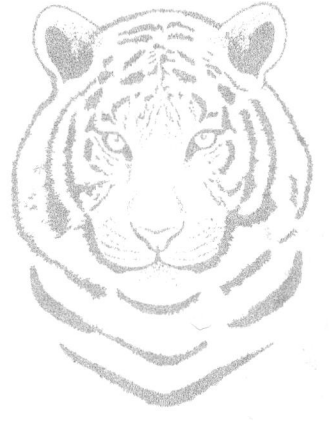

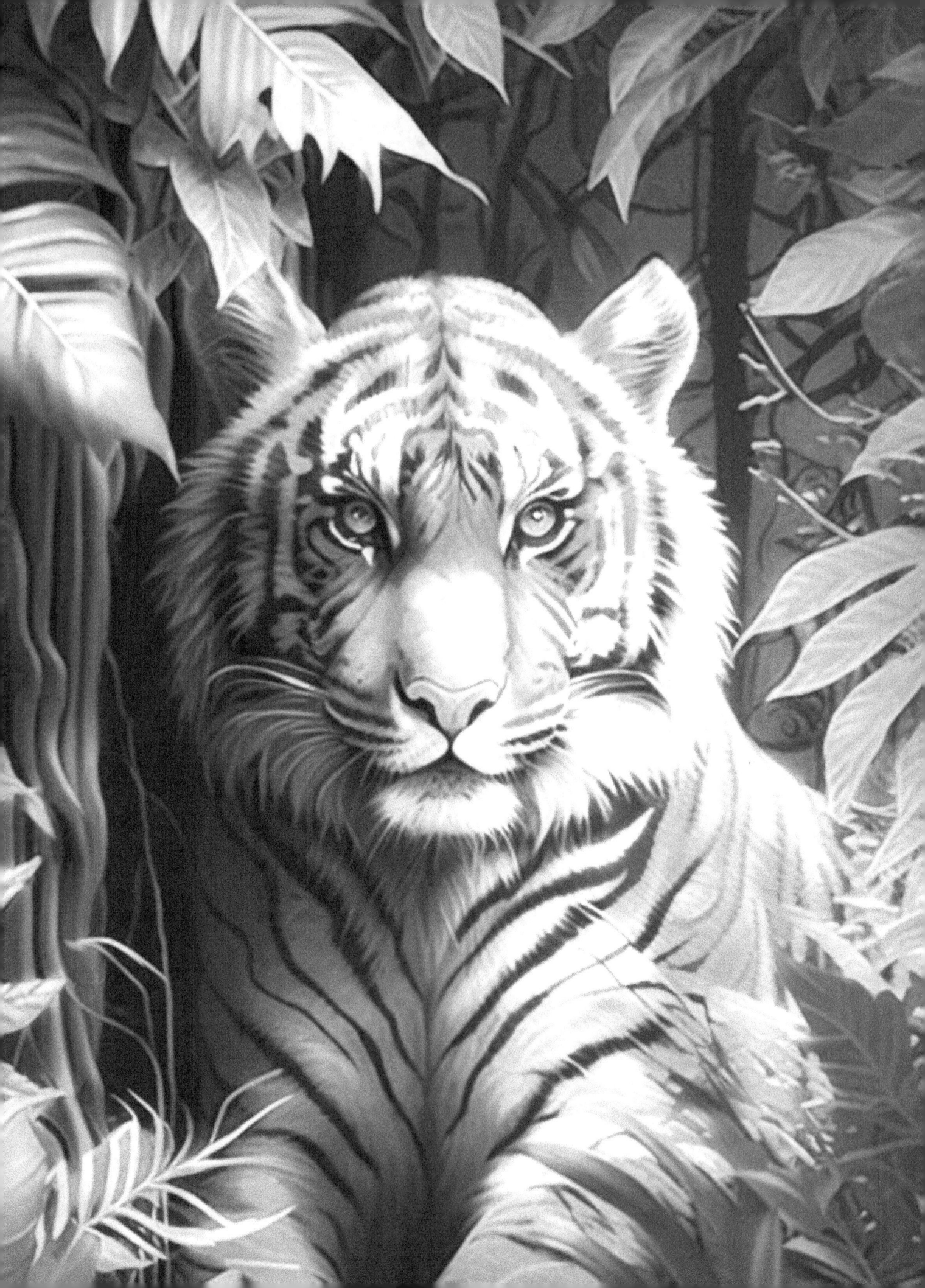

www.ingramcontent.com/pod-product-compliance
Lightning Source LLC
Chambersburg PA
CBHW081659220526
45466CB00009B/2823